Call Me Tennessee
Copyright 2011, Stephen Clements
Edited by Stephen Clements
Experienced Edition

A publication of
Langhorne Creative Group

For more information on this and other LCG publications,
friend Langhorne Creative Group on Facebook and X, and
visit Stephen at @stephen.clements on YouTube and
Rumble at https://rumble.com/c/StephenClements
for dramatic readings of this and other stories.

All the stories presented in this book are true.
Except when they aren't.

Names and trademarks mentioned throughout this book
are the property of their respective owners, and
no challenge is made to their ownership.

Introduction

When I sat down to record my life's tale, I was unsure of the consequences of telling the whole saga. It was only after I sat down and read it, did I realize that I was gaining something else by unveiling to the rest of the world my rather bleak past. I gained a sense of freedom that I had not felt in years, and the anxiety I had been covering up for most of my life seemed to slowly disappear.

This being said, I have decided to air my dirty laundry, despite the almost certain drama that will occur as a result. I realized I spent most of my life running from my greatest fear. I had never feared death: in fact I often looked forward to it in a strange, masochistic way. Despite not having many worldly possessions, I never feared losing them all or never having anything anymore. I had been running away not from my past, nor the present.

I feared life. I feared caring for anything. I feared others being dependent on me for anything. In my mind, fear is the mother of all fuck ups, so if I had nothing or nobody to live for, if I had nothing to lose, I could be fearless. But being fearless always left me with a guilty conscience. I had a guilty conscience for having nothing to lose. I knew I must be missing something.

It took me a while to figure out that sex, drugs, and rock 'n' roll weren't the answers. I thought maybe the answer to life was more of a spiritual thing. That led me to a mental breakdown, so I retreated to the hardcore lifestyle to which I had grown accustomed. I did that just in time to find that all of the people who I had known were either dead or married. The ones that died were always rather tragic deaths, and those who married appeared to have lost their minds.

This just led to me wishing for my own demise, and that is where I appeared to be stranded. Then it seemed to hit me one day while telling a portion of my tale to some random person, it wasn't that I had no fear. I had plenty of fear for life. Now I'm not afraid of life anymore. Thanks for helping me figure that out.

Don't think I've gone soft, because I'm still going to go down in a hail of bullets, with my mouth full of gin and a Molotov cocktail in my hand.

Chapter 1
A Family in Turmoil

To call my birth a mistake would be a lie. In truth, my birth was an act of desperation on my mother's part to keep a failed marriage together. Well, her plan backfired. Three months after my birth, she was put on a plane with two screaming kids and no return ticket bound for Memphis. Yes, she was told that this was only supposed to be a temporary thing, while my father tied up some loose ends. Twenty years later, he died holding the frayed strands.

Needless to say, being the only kid on the block without a father was kind of rough. In the 1980s, unlike today, there actually was a stigma attached to divorce. At the time, things were still reminiscent of the 40s or 50s; it just wasn't done, especially in the South.

From my earliest memories, I recall having to listen to arguments over the phone that resulted in a boy being told, "Your father doesn't want to talk to you: if he did, he would send us money." It was always about money. Yeah, you could say me and my brother were pawns in a game of checkers, if you asked us. Why checkers, not chess? Because chess has some sense of plan or strategy, while checkers makes no sense. Checkers is just a mess of equally worthless pieces running all willy-nilly at each other across the board.

My brother was roughly three by the time he became aware that he would probably never see his father again. He's insisted on blaming me for this in his own mind, which is reflected in his actions. I was born just to keep mom and dad together, and so it was my fault when it failed. I recall, one time I had just fallen asleep, and my brother found a big belt. I woke up with blood running down my face. Several stitches later, I was home, but forever sleeping with one eye open.

Not to say that we only hated each other. We used to have some good, old-fashioned fun, back when kids used to do that sort of thing. There was this grocery store that we frequented, and they had all these gum ball machines. It shouldn't have mattered what the store had, since we were broke, but, while playing with the machine, I discovered that if I pushed here and pulled up there, all the gum balls would come spilling out! He'd be ready to grab up all the gum balls he could get, and I'd help before a worker at the grocery would come try to stop us. So yes, we had some fun. And we fought. We're brothers, that's what we do.

Now, since discipline was somewhat of a concern to my mother, and she was more into shrill screaming and bitter guilt-trips kind, she saw fit to force my grandfather into the mix, for the old-fashioned kind of laying down the law. Her parents, Lenny and Adele, were wonderful people, and they had Nickelodeon back when we only had that black and white television that picked up five channels.

I would often fake falling asleep on their couch to avoid having to go home and sleep in the roach-infested apartment in which we lived. My brother and I had this wonderful game we used to play: after bombing the house for bugs, we would race to the bathroom and see who could count the most roaches in the bathtub.

Running amuck was my own way of escaping the miseries of the cold winters and hot summers in Memphis. I was the black sheep of the family, you could say. I was a 5 year-old kid cursing like a sailor and fighting to stay up to watch Carson's monologue before I went to bed. This made me come across as kind of strange. I had seven cousins at the time, and, by far, I was the most eccentric of the lot. I learned very young that the rules didn't apply to me. This was not because I was spoiled, but the punishment handed out by the law wasn't anything worse than what I was used to.

Now my grandparents were wonderful people, and normally I was on my best attempt at behavior around them, for they gave me a pretty stable home, when I was lucky enough to be there. When I wasn't in that happy place, I spent most of my early years living in my own imaginary world, to get away from the now medically-diagnosed mad hysteria of my mother. That imaginary world, from which I was convinced that I had been switched at birth, I wanted to stay in. Let's face it, my world sucked, but in the fantasies of my own mind, anything was possible.

Since my mother often worked, we had baby sitters, and they preferred to lock us in a closet, rather than keep an eye on us. I recall one lady in particular: she was a fat, black woman that liked to smoke and steal clothes from mother's closet. Well, because of her hefty disposition, she was no match for the wriggling speed of my brother and mine's scrawny little asses: we were able to elude her and raise a little hell. For example, while my brother ran left, I would go right with crayons, markers, and my head to redecorate the walls.

We were such horrid little shits that she left within 10 minutes of her arrival. She would come back, though. Even though she would leave us unattended for absurd amounts of time, we would always tell my mother that she just left.

I recall running up and down the bowling alley on league night, as the babysitter at the alley could not stop me from being a walking tornado. Yeah, I was that kid.

I was always a little hyper, so outside was where I wanted to be. Hell, anybody would rather be anywhere other than in that nasty apartment that reminds you of just how hard life was. I recall one winter, when I awoke in the middle of the evening to relieve myself. To my surprise, the water in the toilet was frozen solid. Let's just say, that winter the three of us became very close.

After we got out of that hellhole, life eased up a little when we moved into a house that a nice lady had offered us at a very low price. This was good, because mom never had any money. Still doesn't. But for the first time, I had my own room, a backyard, and other kids in the neighborhood to play with!

Or so I thought. Soon, I discovered that since my father didn't live with us, none of the kids in the neighborhood would even consider playing with me. This made me kind of bitter, as it seemed my only friend was a mean, old afghan hound with dreadlocks that would have made most hippies proud.

Now Sidney was a violent dog, who taught me the important life lessons of marking your territory and how to protect yourself. He wasn't one to bow to any human authority, and so neither was I. We would play sweet games together, like the "let his crazy ass loose to chase all the kids on the block, and I pretend to try to catch him" game. Soon people learned that I was not to be messed with.

I would play in the back yard to the point that I was more comfortable playing fetch with the dog and talking to myself than dealing with people. The rest of my days were joy-filled with the endless task of procuring food and the occasional toy from whatever store we happened to be shopping in at the time. Let's just say, I was less concerned with putting things in the basket than under my shirt.

Sidney was truly the only one I considered to be family. I had cousins, aunts, uncles, a mom, a dad I barely remembered, even a brother, but no family. I did my best to get along with my cousins at dinner on Friday nights at my grandparents' house, but I was blamed for everything to the point that I was convinced the "D" in my middle name stood for "Damn it!"

I remember the first conversation I had with my father, but not much of it. I didn't know if I should be excited, or mad, or what. I recall asking him what he looked like. He told me he looked like the mailman. Interesting point, the mailman that came to our house was black. Now if being poor and Jewish wasn't hard enough, now I was black, too.

It was assumed by most in the family that I would probably be in jail or dead before age 15. I figured it would happen by 30, so I guess life is just full of surprises. I'm not really sure which one of us wanted that to come true more. For the most part, my cousins were smart, well-mannered, and embarrassed at the very sight of me. I knew from early on that I was going to do something great, just to spite them all.

My mother tried to bring some men around to help influence my brother and I. Most of them meant well enough. They tried their best. They'd talk to us, play with my brother and me, teach us things. One guy named Irwin was nice enough to let me pump gas for his car. Once. See, on accident, I left the pump in the car when we drove off. Good thing was, Irwin was completely insane, so it made for quite a laugh as we sped off into the night.

My mother loved Irwin, like that, but she was afraid of the fact that he liked to drink. And do drugs. Especially the kind that used sharp objects to help set the mood. Oh, and guns. Especially AK-47s, which he took to Cordova, before anybody lived there, and fired off at construction sites. Irwin had a lot of money and no qualms about using it to have a good time, all legal issues being irrelevant to him. He loved my mother like my father never did. But that didn't happen, and she was probably the only thing that slowed him down from his eventual overdose.

His good friend David, who would stop by unannounced just to hangout, was also a cool cat, still is. He was talented, played piano, and the best part of all was he had a motorcycle. One time, he stopped by on his cruiser when I was home alone. He smiled at me, I looked at the bike, and that's all that needed saying. That's right, ladies and gents, we went for a joy ride. Upon our triumphant return two hours later, I saw my mother on the phone with the cops, convinced I had run away. We both couldn't be that lucky.

This final story I will relay from my earliest of memories was of a Tuesday morning. I was sitting down at the table eating a bowl of Franken Berry cereal, and my brother decided he wanted some. I remembered the time he hit me in the face with the belt, and said, "Okay, let me get the milk."

I got the milk out of the fridge, and it somehow managed to fling itself all over his head and the floor, in a karmic act of revenge. Revenge, it's not just for dinner anymore.

That's when mom came out, yelling and screaming that she was never going to buy milk again, because we were both sons of bitches, and we didn't have any more food stamps left. I had never realized how poor we were until the next day, when I looked in the fridge and saw a box of baking soda and a bottle of ketchup. The pantry held a packet of Kool-Aid and a bag of Fritos.

Mom said, "That's all we have until next Friday when I get paid." Actually, wait, I didn't do her justice. You need to understand how she is. So that's when mom said, "THAT'S ALL WE HAVE UNTIL NEXT FRIDAY WHEN I GET PAID."

For the next five days, I remember rationing out how many Fritos I could have, counting them over and over again, like Scrooge McDuck did with all of his gold. The funny thing about poverty is that once you have your food and shelter, you feel like the richest man alive. True, I never really wore new clothes (most of them were my brother's or charity donations from my mother's friends). I never really asked questions where my clothes came from; I was just thankful for the shoes that didn't hurt.

This isn't to say that my mother was a bad person, or that she didn't love us. Rather that she had a very hard time supporting us at time when President Reagan wasn't out to help feed the poor. He was on a mission to put an end to communism.

You see, my mother believed in President Reagan, because he was the governor of California while she lived there. I suppose she felt like they had a connection which she had to hold onto. She constantly sent him letters, asking for help in receiving the child support payments that never came. It was lost on her that Reagan was into self-reliance, and she was asking him for more food stamps.

Life wasn't easy, but for the most part, I had a good childhood. I didn't have much, but I had a good imagination to keep me occupied. At the age of 6, my brother was given the opportunity to visit our father, while I was left at home to deal with my mother, who at this point began to lose most of her sanity. Her oldest son was gone, and she was slowly starting to blame me for all the problems in her life, whether she knew it or not.

Soon after my brother's return, he picked up even more hatred for me, for causing the separation. I was a kid; I didn't do anything to cause two adults to divorce. But that was the only reason I was made, in their eyes. I felt that I had been exiled from my own family. I still feel that way. At this point, I felt alone and realized I could do nothing right, so I might as well raise some hell or die trying. Why not?

Nobody would notice.

Chapter 2
My Early Education

Due to certain elements beyond my control, namely being cruelly both Jewish and poor, my brother and I were enrolled at the Jewish school. Most people would say, "This would give these two unprivileged youths a chance at success in the world!" It wasn't easy for me to blend in there. The stigma attached to couples that divorced was similar to leprosy: people were afraid of you, like divorce was some kind of contagious disease.

I recall in kindergarten, getting into a fight with another boy; the other boy had started it, but I was the one placed in detention. Later, I realized his father had donated a large sum to have the computer lab updated. I struggled to understand the concept of nap time or recess: I figured if I was tired, I would sleep; if I wanted to play I would play: who's a teacher to tell me what to do?

Around this time I began watching movies, all kinds, good, bad, stupid, whatever was on TV. By now, I've made it through every Netflix on-demand movie there is. My love of movies, when combined with my imagination, led me to pretend I was these random characters, to the point that I would be in class and refuse to answer the teacher at roll call, unless my name for the day was called. Needless to say, this didn't go over too well with the authorities.

A little later during recess, I discovered that while no one was watching, I could just walk on home. After doing so for about a week straight, a teacher asked when I was going to stop getting in trouble and attend her class later that day. That's when I realized nobody really missed me. To keep things under the radar, I began making random appearances in her class. But I found out I was right: what with my insubordination in all the other classes, the teachers weren't sad that I wasn't around.

I felt rather uncomfortable there for many reasons, but the most obvious was my lack of school supplies. This one time there was a math competition where two lines were formed, and both students were asked a multiplication question. For my part, I was quicker with the answers, but my reluctance to use paper and pencil was a problem for the teacher. The finals came around, and it was me versus the girl whose grandfather owned most of the city. Not only was I disqualified for not using pencil and paper to show my work, but I got placed into the resource classes to boot.

I learned very young to never let anybody know just how smart you, for they will use it against you. I recall being upset with the school for not letting me participate in recess one day, so like most children I threw a tantrum. Well, the school called in most of the maintenance staff to hold me down, five grown men versus a kid. The difference between them and me was that I was fearless and had nothing to lose, and I won that battle, hands down.

The administration had enough of me, and so about this time it was decided that I would be better suited for public school. People paid their money for their kids to have a nice place to send their little shits to look good and be better than those who couldn't afford it, not to get harassed by a charity case like me. Understand, public school was something new to me: it was hard enough fitting in at my old school for being poor and not having a father, what was this going to be like?

It was awkward being the only person I knew at the school, but what the heck? Things might be different! My optimism lasted all of 10 minutes. As the teacher called the roll, she got to my name and started to struggle, so I corrected her. She looked up at me and said, "You killed Jesus, so sit down and shut up." It would be years before I even met a guy named Jesus, so this tormented me to no end.

I was confronted by a bully who said, "You killed Jesus!" I responded by saying, "If I killed your god, guess what I could do to you?!" Then I kicked him in the groin and punched him in the nose. I then got to meet the principal, who informed me that I was in big trouble, and that I could get a paddle or be sent home. I opted for the paddle, but soon realized the error of my ways.

A few more fights, and I was placed in the special kids class, with the idea that more attention from teachers would lead to less fights. They didn't realize that I had no respect for any of my teachers, because they kept telling me to read instead of actually teaching me. They tried to get me to learn from a book, instead of telling me anything useful. They had this "magic star" system, which never interested me.

One morning before school started, I got into a fight, and the principle informed me I was to wait inside the office every morning until class started. Soon, I caught the attention of the lady who ran the book store. She asked me if I wanted to do something instead of sitting there like a bump on a log. I figured, what the heck, and manned up. I did odd jobs for her, and I impressed her by using my mad math skills to make change without using the calculator she gave me.

I began to behave myself a bit, not for them, but just not to be bothered. Fights still occurred, but so did people calling me fat and making fun of my hand-me-downs. I got my lunch through the free lunch program at the school, but I got most of my food from the younger kids. I wasn't a bully so much as a bodyguard, and this was protection money, not tribute. To say I was bully would be a bit harsh, considering I was constantly verbally assaulted for my weight. Before you think I'm just making stuff up or exaggerating, by high school I weighed over three hundred pounds. That kind of fat doesn't happen overnight. Most women can only manage the freshman fifteen, and the overachievers the freshman fifty.

It wasn't really a cake walk making friends: I wasn't allowed to play with the whites, because I was Jewish; I couldn't play with the blacks, because I looked white; the Jews wouldn't play with me, because I was poor. Soon after, I realized the only way I would make it was with respect, so rather than studying, I chose to fight for my respect. Winning and losing had nothing to do with it; it wasn't personal, just for respect. Needless to say, my fighting didn't stop at school: it took place everywhere, from Boy Scouts to synagogues.

I didn't enjoy hurting people, I just enjoyed letting them know I could. It got to the point where I realized I had nothing to lose by acting out and nothing to gain by playing it straight. I must say, however, no matter how bad the fights were, weapons like guns and knives were never thought of: we settled it with our fists.

As far as school work, it got done. I would race the class to see who could finish assignments first, and most of the time I won.

Homework was done if there was nothing on TV, or if it was raining, or my grandfather would force me to do it before he took me out to dinner. I never gained much from homework; I always thought it was useless, just like class work. In fact, to this day I believe I learned more watching TV and movies than I ever picked up in any class, no matter what the topic was.

My experiences in life made it so that there were no expectations for me to meet, and most people figured that I'd drop out or work in some factory screwing the caps on bottles. My brother was still at the Jewish school and wasn't much help when it came to anything really, except he could cook a mean dinner. I once took an IQ test, and I took my time to make sure I missed everything. I was told a pidgin had a higher learning potential than me, and with that I was forced in to resource classes again and told to visit a doctor in order to help out with my psyche.

At graduation, I was forced to carry the American flag for the ceremony in full Boy Scout uniform. There was one slight problem: as I was preparing to bring the flag in, I discovered my zipper was broke. Unsure of how to cover it up or to limit my embarrassment, I simply tucked my shirt in and pulled it through my fly. I know, it looked as stupid as it sounds, but it made sense at the time. There are still people to this day upset with me for disrespecting the flag. I meant no disrespect, but I was a kid trying to avoid embarrassment the only way I knew: through a little humor.

I learned that when some people don't get a joke, they believe you have issues and need to be placed on medication, in order to control your bizarre behavior. I made my way through my elementary school with one thought: just get out of this place. It smelled funny, and anywhere has got to be better.

One thing that does stick out was a fight I had at the end of third grade, with a kid by the name of Clarence. Normally this would not bother me, except that over the summer, he jumped into one of his neighbor's pool. Unfortunately for him, the pool had no water in it, and he died. After this, I made it a point to be civil towards those I was accustomed to fighting. My disrespect for teachers grew, though, as

13

they refused to answer my questions that had good points, but they thought were incoherent.

Around the age of 8, I got to meet my father for the first time, when me and my brother flew to California. I was unsure of many things, but I soon learned that most of the things my mother told me weren't exactly true, but rather slightly exaggerated. When I got back to Memphis from the summer away, I realized how much life sucked in Memphis and how much cooler my life would be in California, living with my father.

I started acting out in strange ways, like sleeping under my bed with the hopes that people would think I ran a way in the middle of the night. One replaying memory in my mind was when my brother and I pissed off the woman we called mom, and she threw a package of frozen hotdogs at us. Luckily, my cat-like reflexes kicked in, and I dodged the flying dogs, but the window wasn't nearly as lucky. Of course, since it was my mom, me and my brother were blamed for physically forcing her to throw the damn hotdogs at us.

I hate to make it seem like I was physically abused growing up. In truth, I was abused, but it was mostly the psychological abuse Jewish mothers are so good at. The grandparents were cool. When I misbehaved too badly, I was forced to ride with my grandfather on his sales calls through a bunch of one-horse towns in Mississippi and Arkansas. Talk about a boring trip: the most fun I had was collecting rocks, while he was inside playing gin in exchange for sales. Now on the weekends, my grandparents and I would sit around and play cards; at one point I won my grandfather's car, but since I wasn't 12 yet, I let him keep it.

I remember hearing the stories of my grandparents and their parents regarding the race riots and the strike that brought the great Martin Luther King, Jr. to Memphis, only to meet his demise. I can tell you that my grandparents had nothing but respect for African-Americans, at times when whites would not hire a Jew or pay a black a decent wage. They would often hire blacks over whites, with the full knowledge that the white supremacists would go after their business. At a time when many Jews only hired family, my grandparents would hire blacks and paid them more than their own family members, because they felt they needed it more.

These were the values I understood and came to believe in, despite the racism inherent in the city of Memphis. You can say I grew up in Memphis at a unique time, when the first black mayor came to power, and the great white flight took place. As an outsider, I understood what was going on, what went on, and what was never talked about.

Chapter 3
Mental Evaluations

Before I enrage people by stating my unique stance on mental health, I will tell you this much: I believe in the words of Jimmy Buffett, that "If we weren't all crazy, we would go insane." Being labeled ADD and ADHD ahead of the modern craze, I was given a couple drugs with conflicting effects, so I can speak with authority to mental health problems in the world. The way I see it, I'm the only sane person on the planet: everybody else is as loony as a fruit cake.

That being said, I was considered a trouble maker, a class clown, a bully, an outsider, call me what you will. I never held a grudge; a fight was a fight, and it ended when it ended. In class, I dreamt of the days gone by that we heard about in history, when men were men, and pride was something to die for. Now grade school fights, bad combinations of behavior-controlling drugs, and the trip to visit my father in California at the age of 8 did little but confuse me as to what the point was of modern times. Were men supposed to be men? Were they supposed to be chicken shits that picked little pellets out of bowls and shat all over themselves? I was all confused, and I wasn't the only one.

The family began going to counseling at a local center, but I acted out when I figured out that the councilors predetermined that my mother was all-knowing and truthful in describing me as the source of all the problems in the family. I was pissed off, rightfully so, but my attitude led to more doctors, more pills, and eventually I was placed in a mental facility.

It was all fun and games in the group therapy sessions. I had yet to hit puberty, and the teenagers in the room were struggling with sex, drugs, and other mental issues, like the kids who were cutting themselves or the guy who was Jonesing for a fix. I was the one who would call people out and mention that they were retarded, or offering the crackhead the idea to turn prostitute for $5 a lay.

Everyone else in there, excluding the staff, knew I didn't belong. I was just a kid with serious problems, not crazy. I didn't roll my shit into little balls and laugh at them. I remember nothing good of this place. They asked me to share my feelings, but then said I was irrational and bizarre.

Now after spending the better half of two years in and out of this facility, I emerged a drugged-up zombie. No feelings, drooling at the mouth for my next dose of lithium and Prozac, and the four other drugs I was on. I was put in that white room you so often hear about, but probably never seen. I can tell you that I would often use the corner to relieve myself, so they would be forced to sanitize the room, which meant they couldn't put me back in the room for a couple of days.

I spent most of my days and nights staring at the walls, trying to plan my escape. In my time in restraints, I managed to slip out of the four on my hands and ankles, but that damn belt just wouldn't have any of it. I spent years under the notion that I was ill because my family said so, and to this day I believe they still think I'm nuts. What was so bizarre about a boy at age 12 or 13 running away from home, or camping in the storage shed, because he didn't want or need his parents to teach him how to live like they did? I did my best to fit in, but never did. Throughout all the counseling and what not, I learned that there are screwed up people in this world, and in their view I was one of them.

My own faults were there. I screwed up, but still, I couldn't have been this first kid kicked out of Boy Scouts for lack of a proper family name. I worked hard at recalling all the details of my life, before trying to take it at the age 13. I went for the gold a couple of times before it was cool, or a way for whiny kids to seek attention. Somehow, I felt my mother would find a way to benefit from all the attention, and like hell I was going to let her get the last word in. All else being equal, if I had the means, I would have offed myself many times over.

Instead, I knew my only chance to keep any of my sanity was to get out, and knowing that I would never be declared sane by the doctors, I had to find another way. I said to myself, "Let's go for the one thing that they would never expect," so I yelled rape. At first, I just yelled that I was getting beaten, and that led to some rather sensitive questions. But I saw that just getting hurt by the people there wasn't going to cut it.

But then the woman questioning me asked if I was abused sexually. I was silent for a minute, and then I went for the waterworks, followed by the silent nod. For someone of my stature, at the time my actions and attention to detail was just unheard of. Nowadays, kids come equipped with scripts to handle this situation, but I had to wing it. I alleged that a staff member tried to rape me, and within twelve hours, I was home in my own bed.

What a whirlwind that was. I was still playing a saved video game in my head. I was forced into more psycho drama, but it was different this time: I was the one with the power. I learned their tricks and picked up a few of my own along the way, at least enough to fake it. It took me a while to come clean, but when I did nobody ever questioned my sanity again. I did what I did to survive. I'm a Mother Fucking Survivalist™! Yeah, people got hurt, but I survived, and that's really all that counted.

I was sent to a school for retards and rich drug addicts who had issues. I proved myself not mentally retarded, but I was extremely socially unacceptable. Despite being obese, smelling really bad, and having the luck of extremely bad timing when telling jokes, I made a few friends. It was only through exercising all my power and determination was I able to get out of that damn place. I knew I had to separate myself from that kid who ate his brownies with the plastic wrapper still on.

You read that right. I asked why he did it like that once. "So that it lasts longer." Now I asked myself, how the hell did I get here, and then I realized every stunt that I pulled, all the things I was doing to be cool really weren't working. I really didn't have any friends, and I was stuck in this school for retards.

I recall transferring to another city school mid-year. When I got there, the rumors circulated that I was a pyromaniac. Now I was still big on defending my honor, and ass-kicking was still served on the menu. I walked out of an art class on my first day, and had I not held my book up fast enough, my nose might have been broken. Had I not used my book as a hammer before pushing some wanna be gangsta into a locker, I would have had a rather rough time at my new school.

My second day, some kid walked up to me at lunch, said, "You think your hot shit, don't you?", and spit on my lunch. So I got up, threw the lunch in his face, and just then I was restrained by one of the monitors in the lunch room, who pulled me to the side of the cafeteria. Which also happened to have a pile of 2x4s lying around.

So I picked one up and made my way over to apologize by slapping this punk in the back of his head with it. I was stopped and told I could be expelled, and I told the monitor he had no idea who the hell I was. I broke the 2x4 over that kid's head and then made my way out past the baseball fields to the catwalks, where all the cool kids smoked. I made that my own personal classroom for a good month, until I got suspended. I guess I was at that school maybe five full days in my three months in attending such a fine institution.

It might have been cruel to accept cigarettes in exchange for a proper beat-down of some kid, but I'll be damned if that was my only flaw. I did what I had to. I make no excuses, just letting you in on my reasoning. You did buy my book; I figure you deserve that much.

I was a big enough asshole to get the school administration to kick me out, because, well, I didn't want to be there anymore than they did. So it was back to the retard school. I was out of place, out of time, and most of all out of patience for those posers. I learned it was nothing more than I didn't fit in, and that I should accept that I will never fit in.

Keep in mind, when I came back from California before entering 8th grade, I had just been to a football camp, where I was the guy everybody wanted to know. I had just played tennis for the first time, and the beginners couldn't hang with me. I knew who I was: I was the kid whose father left him at the laundromat for a few hours to play video games, while he got ripped at the bar down the road.

Only upon my finding a highway patrolman and telling him my dad dropped me off here and I don't know where he lives, nor his phone number, did I get picked up and sent to my uncle, who had a beautiful house on Malibu beach. It was there where the girl with the red hair came and saved me from drowning. It was there much later on, after a party invite and a six pack of beer, that I lost my virginity.

After being the man in California, at least in my mind, I came back to Memphis and realized I was just some punk kid. This might mean I was depressed; go figure, I had no choice. I loved the Beach Boys, Jimmy Buffett, and the Grateful Dead at that time, and nobody caught my drift. I was a legend in my own mind, but located somewhere that made me nothing more than a court jester.

Chapter 4
Adolescence

I'm not quite sure what to write about here. I had no life, no friends, I stayed awake all night listening to 8-tracks of Jimmy Buffet and the Rolling Stones, and praying to the moon gods. I for the most part cared nothing for society, people, or anything to do with normalcy.

I started working at the age of 13, putting boxes together and filling orders for a small business. A few years later, I began working in a restaurant for cash on the side; nothing pretty, just washing dishes and mopping floors. I called myself the cleanup supervisor. My brother, the talented chef, got me the job, and I kept it to stay out of the house. I remember washing dishes one day, and the cook asked me what I was doing scraping the bottom outside of the pan. I told her, "If I'm going to do something, I'm going to do it right."

I also needed the cash for the weekend poker games with the rich, smart kids I was associated with through AZA, a Jewish high school fraternity of sorts. Yeah, it was great: we had formals, and the girls had to say yes. Of course, I always asked the hottest or most popular ones out. It still did nothing for me: I had no joy, no pain, and I still felt like a zombie, only without the drugs.

Don't get me wrong, we had tons of fun as the last generation to get away with playing tackle football on the weekends. Had it not been for the people I met or the friends I made in AZA, I would have killed myself. Aside from that, I had no life, so I went to everything, from basketball games to a regional convention, and I made myself known early and often.

Early on in the AZA, I had problems fighting and what not. Had it not been for the chapter advisor, one Andrew Todd Forman, I would have continued my actions, but he didn't take sides. He told it to me straight, and I got it. He told me something as simple as, "Stop letting these guys get to you. What they heck do they know any better than you how to be cool?" I started to accept the things I couldn't change, and while I didn't like it, I dealt with it. I learned to have fun bending the rules without breaking them.

After my year at the retard school, I transferred back to public school, which happened to be the optional magnet school in the city. Before my attendance could be approved, I had to have a meeting with one assistant principle, who asked me to play by the rules and avoid trouble. To ensure this, I was to meet her in her office every morning to make sure I had no beefs with anybody, and to keep me from getting into any fights before school. In light of my history, it made good sense to me.

The only problem was she had another student with a history of drug sales doing the same thing, only she searched his person and bag for drugs. After day two, it was, "What are you doing here?", and we became good friends. We swapped backpacks for the purpose of the search, and in exchange I got two hits of acid per day. This made school interesting for the first time in my life!

Yeah, I was nervous at first, but my paranoia went away with time, and I really got into learning for the first time. Somehow, after kicking all the prescription drugs, the acid helped me concentrate. Even better, while I maintained a steady B average, I remained out of sight and out of mind of the authorities. I was finally doing things right. Thanks, Acid!

After a while, I quit the acid and just took a twenty spot instead. Now the lunch room came upon me as a unique opportunity to socialize with the smart kids and get my homework done in minutes, as opposed to the idea of studying all night. Fuck that.

I did this for about a year, and then one day the football coach walked up to me and said, "I heard you're crazy." I told him opinions varied and that I had learned to control myself. He asked me if I wanted to play again, and, well, how could I say no to a tobacco-chewing, good ole boy with a son named Nathan Bedford?

To set the mood for a lot of my high school years, my last name was Klitzner, and I was a big kid, coming in at six feet, 320 pounds. That landed me the nickname of "Big Klit". At first, I hated the name, then I realized it had stuck, and all hell could be fought and it wouldn't change a damn thing. So I did what anyone would do: I embraced the name, and when some shouted, "Hey, Big Klit!", I responded with a smooth, "What up, G?!"

So midway through my junior year, I started lifting weights and goofing off, starting at around six in the morning with about twelve other guys. Most of them were popular and wanted to spend time after school hanging out with their girlfriends, instead with a bunch of sweaty guys. Me, I worked after school, so I would buy my lunch before school and eat something other than burnt rectangular pizzas.

The coach pulled me aside one day and asked me to take this one guy under my wing, and get him talking to people. You read that right, I was normal compared to this guy. Since I appeared to be kind of hip in coach's eyes, I took Lunch Box under my wing. Let me describe Lunch Box for you: he was wide as a chimney, blonde, and docile. Sure, he was built like a gorilla and could probably snap you in half, but that would never occur to him to do that. I figured if nothing else, our lunch table would be the scariest-looking in the cafeteria.

I invited him to my table of geeks, and soon we took control of the table. With our anti-Christian attitudes combined, we managed to shock enough people to get warned that our religious speech rights were limited in school. I soon became accepted in most circles at a school full of cliques. I was a bit of a redneck-hippie-Jew, a combination that turned my life upside down and twice removed from all purposeful circles. I was accepted as an outsider who could run inside, but I didn't try to, so it was just a natural progression for me. Funny, all that time trying to fit in, and all I had to do was not care about fitting in and give everybody else the "what the hell is wrong with you" look. Intimidation was no longer my game so much, as I didn't give a rat's ass about you or your rules; I'm doing it my way.

My reputation for being a fighter never left me, despite being fight-free for a while. I got by, made my own way, learned to bend rules, and even fought my way out of resource and into standard classes. It wasn't a big struggle, despite what some might think; it was more of just emulating who the teachers were and writing the way they would talk. In other words, using their style of speech and general attitude about life in my school work would get me passing grades.

This is something I wish to pass on, in the lesson of coasting. In order to coast, you must hit the ground running, work hard early on, and then you can do whatever you want, just stay in the lane. You're welcome.

For the record, it's not cheating if you don't get caught: think of it as academic outsourcing. Note to the younger readers: never cheat off the Asian kid, he will always rat on you. Also, be mindful of the person you're comparing answers to, make sure they are smarter than you. When trying to cheat, always do it in the open. After a while, the teacher will think it's impossible to be that stupid and let you slide.

Anyways, working, AZA, and football were enough to keep me out of trouble. I did my time and then some: I worked hard in and out of school, to the point that free time was a novelty. I wondered how people did the whole work thing all their lives. From what I could tell, nobody liked working, and to be honest, it was a pain in the ass. I was working hard and only getting a couple of dollars a night. It wasn't a lot of money, and it would never be enough money, but it was better than nothing.

At this point, I had some friends who let me sleep over at their houses and call their moms mom. People knew I was crazy, but they just blamed it on my parents. It was strange: people who knew my situation pitied me, and those that didn't thought I was good to go.

Chapter 5
Senior Year

As you can imagine by now, my senior year was on cruise control, at least until three weeks in, when the administration reread the guidelines for graduation. Turns out, I needed some extra classes, easy ones, like chemistry, geometry, and algebra II. I was supposed to be coasting, damn it!

I lucked out in algebra II and chemistry, with teachers who thought that I was above cheating. I had various methods, like "accidentally" stapling the answer sheet to the work sheet, but my personal favorite was when my chemistry teacher called me out for staring at the chest of the girl who sat in front of me during a test. She was nice enough to share the answers with me, and the teacher pulled me out of class to explain that if I liked the girl, I should ask her out. That worked for a while.

So eventually, the stress of taking real classes played itself out. I had also gotten lucky with Spanish II: I had a fat teacher who nobody respected, let alone listened to. My friends Brad, Jeremy, and me spent most of our time playing paper football, sometimes until our fingers bled. One girl did the work and passed it around for the class to enjoy.

My English teacher hated me for the first part of the year. I figured that out when she called me an illiterate jerk. Words like that make a guy feel he's special. But she was right. I've spent years trying to prove her wrong. Later, I convinced the assistant principle who had reread the requirements for graduation to transfer me into the class of the English teacher I had the year before.

I had my run of the school, with a crew of jocks and Jews. I had nothing to prove. I was living high during football season. We had our downs, but we won a game that happened to be on Yom Kippur. That also meant that I, as a Jew, played the game without drinking water. I'm no Sandy Koufax, but I went to temple the next day. I got a call from the paper while getting ready for temple, and I gave them enough quotes that, for the next practice, the coach called me a superstar.

In fact, my best memory came in a loss to our rival at the time. I was damned convinced I wasn't going to play, because I had goofed off during practice. By the second half, my thigh pads were hanging down around my knees, because I just knew there was no way I was playing. Coach had been pissed at me all week. Sure enough, the coach yelled at me, "Get in there and do something!"

So I went in against some third-string offensive guard and just ran over him. I jumped over the center and hit quarterback. He still got the pass off, but it was dropped, and I got mad props in the film session after the game. I even got to start that next week. I was told on the bus that I'd be going "Ironman" that game. It was rough losing games, but I gave it my all, and it still kinda sucked.

One day, I passed the wrestling coach and joked with him about going out for the team. Me being 50 pounds over the max weight, I thought he would let it go. Next week, I joked with the kicker on the football team about going out for wrestling, and he made so much fun of me for it, even betting me $50 I would never make weight. So I went for it, trying all kinds of diets, like working out wearing trash bags under my sweats, even over spring break, trying to cut the weight.

I finally lost the weight and made the squad, and, well, I lost my first match, second match and the third match I should have won, but I got cocky and lost. For me, it was the workouts, the team work in a sport of individuals, and I found it to be more of a team effort than anything else. Even today, I defend those who sweat with me and will never forget those that made it possible. Thanks, Coach Fuller, for teaching me about hard work and self-confidence.

I hate hard work, but I will never let anybody tell me that I can't do something. Self-confidence is a sense of pride that no one can take from you, but you can give it away. I learned more that year about me than I've ever forgotten. Now, for all my troubles, I stayed clean up until I got a board suspension for writing "Fuck You" on a pop quiz. Then came that uppity girl in my class who couldn't take a joke, and after writing love notes to her, I got tired of seeing them ripped up, so I just started passing blank notes to her.

I got called to the principal's office and flat-out told him, "Look, I like her, but the notes are more of a joke, because she gives such priceless reactions!" Later, her mom came up to me at the sports banquet and laid into me, apparently under the impression that I was somebody it was easy to intimidate. At this banquet, I was being a good boy, though, so I just smiled and looked at her tits. I tried to avoid attention, but like a bull in a china shop, my exploits were known. I even got a standing ovation, because I came in second place for the Wrestler of the Year Award, just for my dedication.

Like in most things that year, I got a lot of praise for determination. I had respect from many at the AZA convention, and I got nominated for president by a peer as a joke. I made an impromptu speech in which I vowed to repeat my senior year if elected, and then I reminded people that it wasn't a popularity contest. Then as now, you should vote for the most qualified person, and then I took myself out of the race (I still came in third place).

I had my run for the ages with the great football games on Sundays with the crowd. My superior athletics led me to break a kid's nose, allegedly, but it was all gravy. I even gained popularity at another high school. I will say this: I hope my rivals in life have the same regard for me as I do them.

I never realized how much fun, or trouble, could be had until I turned 18. I had a collection of posters on my walls that would make Charlie Sheen happy. I soon learned that Hooters and strip clubs were much better wastes of money than a poker game with a bunch of other dudes. I recall a senior luncheon, at which me and a few hombres decided to move it to the local Hooters. A group of cops were there, and they thought it was cool enough to let us slide on the whole skipping school thing.

Now my summer came up quick. With my destination unknown, I took a job at the game room of the local Jewish Community Center, and used my superior lighting skills to set up a debate for the local Rotary Club. To quote myself, "If I could remember the times they said we had, then I would be a wise man. Since I can't, I'll just nod alongside at the stories you tell." I learned a lot watching all those old dudes talk about their fat stacks and charities. That was where I met a guy from TV, who got me interested and on the path of studying mass communications, my eventual college major.

At the same job, there was a chick I thought was hot who would come and pick up her brother. I got up the nerve to ask her out, only to find out she was just 14. And that was my luck at the time.

Chapter 6
Freshman Year

I don't know much, but what I do know is that crap on the radio at the time sucked, so I got into classic rock. I remember the ride up to college with my big brother from Big Brothers and Big Sisters. We talked over what I should expect in college, but I had no clue what I was in store for. I was lost, bouncing my tennis ball for hours against the wall on move-in day, met my neighbors, then just turned up the radio with the door open, waiting for someone to notice me.

The shit worked! I met the two guys across the hall from me: one was named Duck and I can't remember the other one. The important part was that they were ATO's. Now, I had no intention of joining a frat when I went to college, but boredom is a bitch, and parties made sense. So I went through rush, had a blast, and my heart was set on ATO, but little did I know what would happen.

I wasn't sure of much except that I hated the Pikes. Most people turned a blind eye to the fat guy, so I wasn't sure if anybody would extend a bid to me. A group known as Tau Kappa Epsilon caught my eye, and I theirs. After the laughs passed and the conversations came and went, I actually enjoyed their company more than anybody else. They weren't preppy, rich, snotty, or arrogant at all, which was rare when it came to fraternities.

They stood not for wealth, rank, or honor, but for personal worth and character. That was just what I needed. Unfortunately my cash flow was nonexistent, and aside from a job handing out video cameras for an hour or two a day, I had no cash coming in. I decided to wait until after I learned the ropes and found some work, so I declined the first semester, but accepted the second. I remember a few bits of my course work, and one tidbit was a quote from the late, great W.C. Fields: "I spent all my money on wine, women, and cigars. The rest I squandered."

Now, still being pissed off at that English teacher that called me illiterate, I joined the school paper as a sports reporter. Sure, I had no experience, just a desire. I soon became the go-to guy when it came to sports stories, with the help of my editor Scott Perkins. He aided me and helped me get to a point that one of my stories won second place in the state media awards. I also had a flare for the dramatic and began writing really bad columns. I was the pride and joy of the media family, if you want to say such things.

My brother got married within the first few weeks of me getting to college. Now that was kind of boring, so I'll give you some good stuff before that, for here is where I learned a few lessons in life. Lesson one, my father taught me about hops and how to enjoy beer, and then he explained single malt to me. Second lesson, I learned being a Jew in Arkansas could be a lonely business. My brother helped me carry in a TV after his wedding, with a kippa on his head. He attracted enough attention for everybody to find out I was a Jew, so I was soon invited to church socials and reminded of the fact I killed Jesus on a regular basis.

All in all, I did what most do in college: I drank, skipped some classes, learned when the drop date for classes was, and overslept way too often. I did what I had to, but tried to stay focused. I also found out that the paper staff enjoyed having me around for some reason. Maybe it was the fact that my free time was spent at basketball games, debating sports with reporters from the local paper, and writing and rewriting all my stories. I noticed something in my efforts, that determination is a valuable trait. It turns out that the paper had been paying me as a staff reporter. It wasn't a lot of money, but the next semester it would be more, and I could pick it up at the beginning and end of the semester.

I struggled some in my classes, what with all the partying going on. My philosophy teacher was giving me a hell of a time, and I had a rough time keeping up. I lucked out with his final exam question, "What is the meaning of life?" I wrote a 15-page essay/suicide note. That landed me a surprise phone call from the professor and a meeting with him and a school counselor. It also got me a B, instead of the F I deserved. Others thought my plan was horrible; I called it Darwinism at work.

Next spring, I was forced into study hall by my fraternity, and wouldn't you know it, I got a 3.5 average and approval for every class I wanted. I was even made secretary of my fraternity. I was more OCD than anything else: I worked hard, got help from people along the way, and made it through.

Still limited in what I would call true friends, I was still communicating with folks in Memphis online. I met a fellow named Rooster with his bottle-glasses, who wouldn't stop talking about weed. I was drug-free at the time, and to call marijuana weed was not in my own vocabulary yet. It was going around, and I ignored it. Then came this thing called meth, and I wanted no part of it. People around me were doing it, and others were broken by doing it, and I was busy, too busy for that jibber-jabber.

A few miles down the road at a place called "Jerry's", I learned about beer, steak and Hank Williams, Jr. In fact, if you're ever hung over, listen to "A Country Boy Can Survive": the beats match the beating in your head, and soon enough your hangover is gone.

I also learned a few things that year, when I ventured out to California for Christmas break. I had a great time connecting with family, and also connecting with my aunt and uncle's excellent music collection. I must say, for hippies, they had an extensive collection, even though I'm still an Elvis and blues guy. The Grateful Dead made me question music and what other kinds there were. Thank you Otis Redding, for you have given me more reflection than a mirror in those dark days of my freshman year.

Freedom of expression had long been my purpose in life, and to take that from me might as well have been the knife in my back. I've been thinking about that awesome freshman year, and the defining moment for me came when I wrote a column about a sign somebody had put up on campus and called "art", because of some guy named Robert Frost. My piece merely argued for separation between church and state, but others took it to be an attack on Christianity. This would not have bothered me so much, except I was a little defensive about my own views. To my luck, a student came to my defense when the shit was heating up. His father was governor at the time, but nonetheless, he helped put out the fires. Thank you.

31

True, some people may say I had the life that year. I say it was Hell, and you couldn't pay me to relive the stress of that whole ordeal. It turned out college was a lot harder than I thought, and finding people that I could hang out with even harder. During high school, towards the end I was comfortable, and I had built up somewhat of a rep, depending on who you talk to. But college was like starting from scratch, which for me meant having absolutely nothing.

Chapter 7
Sophomore Blues

Now, this year was important in my development, because this is when I first met my boy Bob, who no matter what I got his back, and I know he's got mine. Second, I got Lunch Box to move up to Jonesboro and go to A-State with me, but both of them have helped me on in my years, and even still today. This was one of those years where I really came out of my shell.

My radio production class was fun, and I would torment my professor with back to back Clapton, followed by Garth Brooks, and end it all with a splash of Rufus Thomas' version of "Walking the Dog". If you don't know it, learn it. Props to Stax Music for all the hits.

Anyway, I excelled in classes where I could express my thoughts and get away with opinionated rants. I also had a teacher who told me that if you don't show up, you'll never pass. To prove a point, I didn't show up, and I got a C- in the class. I had my pick of stories at the paper, and the radio station gave me the 4 am shift, so I did it all. It was a non-profit classical station, so I had issues staying awake. I never got tired of slipping some Clapton or Santana into the mix with all the violins and French horns past the programming director.

I had good fun, but the times were a changing, and so were the politics. I recall joking in 2000 about learning how to fly an airplane, like one of those old Russian jets, and learn just enough to take off and eject before ramming it into the damn library. What can I say, I was ahead of my time!

I began picking up bad habits, like smoking cigarettes and sleeping instead of going to class, but the parties were great. I worked in Memphis on the weekends, putting in 40+ hours, and then driving back for class. That made life interesting. I heard a song one day, and it made sense to me. Then I read a quote of the writer, and I understood more than I should. Yes, I am the walrus. Respect.

Sorry, I don't remember much of this year: that's the bad part of alcohol and living the life of a rock star without the fortune and fame. Life got to be more of a puzzle, and I had to lie to a few professors to

33

get my straight As, what with putting in 40 hours worth of work in two days in Memphis, working the graveyard shift at a radio station, and doing the newspaper thing.

Meanwhile, one of my classes had a girl who was part Indian (feather, not the dot variety). She played basketball, so we knew each other on a professional basis, so to speak. I had dyed my hair blonde one day, but it turned out rather orange, and when combined with the fact that I was 200 pounds overweight, she laughed at me. So I challenged her to a game of one-on-one!

How was I supposed to know that her friends, teammates, and coaches would show up and be cheering her on? I figured it was going to be quiet, just me and her. I got beat in three straight games, and then I said, "Ok, this one's for all the marbles."

Did I mention this girl was close to 6'4" and my 6-foot, fat ass was three minutes from a heart attack? I stepped it up and did what I knew how to do: I took the ball first and nailed five shoots in a row, then somehow managed a steal and got a lay-up, at which point the coach asked if I would wear a dress to get on his team. Then I went for it, hitting my flat-footed jumpers, winning the last match.

Maybe it was pity on her part for the sweaty, wobbling fat-ass about to die on the court with her, but I won and I took the victory, damn it! I miss those girls and boys from the basketball teams: they wore their chips on their shoulders, and you couldn't take it from them.

Meanwhile, I had run for a position on the Residence Hall Association and won. After enough people quit, I had the job of being the national rep for Arkansas State. There was a conference in Tulsa, where the night before elections, I stayed up all night planning a coup to make sure the current president running for reelection would know she had problems. I did the statesman-like thing: argued until my throat hurt, and then let another speak. I was really trying to get this other chick elected, because she seemed cool, and she bought me beer. I figured it was the least that I could do. My attempt failed, but not as bad as you might think: I managed to get her elected as Vice-President, after brokering an agreement with the President.

I kept dying my hair and running around like a chicken with my head cut off. I was on the Residence Hall Association Board, the secretary of my fraternity, a staff reporter, interning at the radio station on campus, working at the book store, and at a hotel in Memphis. Did I mention a full class load? Parties, papers, radio, and a lot of coffee.

Oh yeah, I forgot to mention that I'm dyslexic and really hate reading. I developed my own style of learning, which has a lot more to do with relating to the professors' views and less with reading. I never understood the need to reference in essays, because I prefer the power of individual thought and coming to your own conclusions through whatever means necessary. Who cares that somebody else said something; what the hell do they know?

How I maintained my sanity is the wrong question to ask. You should ask if I was ever sane. Oh yeah, I also mastered Diablo 1, for all you video game freaks out there. Respect.

I made my way through that year, working school activities, going through the motions. For me, it was fun to a point, but eventually I came to the realization that life at this school wouldn't help me much. Maybe it was when I saw a friend who had a graduate degree stocking shelves at Wal-Mart, but I realized that I needed a more academically-centered university. I had been there two long years, and my heart wasn't into conning my professors for the grades I wanted anymore.

I actually had two professors that taught me more about life than any others would: Mr. Fowlers and Mrs. Rodgers, who had a knack for a good story or two, while Mr. Fowlers had a knack for making the book come alive. Also, Dr. Robertson knew more than I ever could about media, and we agreed in principle that P.T. Barnum was the godfather of public relations. Yeah, Hurst had his moments, but let's face it, when the circus comes to town, you're going for no other reason than to be entertained.

At this time, I also fell in love with this stuff called folk rock. Cat Steven's "Another Saturday" hit me in ways that I never thought it could be done. Boy, did I ever enjoy life right then. My brother just had a baby girl named Candace, and I took her with me to buy a present one time. She tried to buy clothes; I bought her an Easter bunny. The baby loved it, and my life was looking up and down at the same time. It's an odd concept, really.

But getting back to college, I got back on the asshole wagon by pulling pranks all over the place. Now I had reasons for all the pranks I pulled, whether it was sticking a rat under the door of the Dorm Director's apartment or refusing to name who the Uni-Shitter was. Or turning the shower heads so they'd fall off when turned on, or placing catfish stink bait in random shampoo bottles. It's a real blast, watching people's faces when they catch a whiff of the dude walking past them, who is thinking other people are to blame, since he just showered.

But I'm sure by now you're saying, "Whoa, Jeff, you can't bring up someone called the Uni-Shitter without explaining that one!" Okay, fine. So the Uni-Shitter, like the Uni-Bomber before him, would drop a load in the shower, and it varied which bathroom would be the scene of the crime day by day. The guys in the residence hall set up a sting operation and failed to catch him. In fact, I was a suspect at one time, but let's face it, the bathrooms were condemnable anyway, so if the man wanted to shit in the shower, who am I to tell him not to?

A lot of things went wrong that semester, but my collection of parking cones grew, as the campus cops tried to block parking spots in order to put in meters. I just took all the cones and put them in my trunk. Sticking it to the man became harder and harder under the watchful eyes of the local authorities.

I started a unique uprising when my column about how nasty the dormitories were came out: I made enemies, and, somehow, the financial aid department magically started losing documents of mine that they already had on file. Like my selective service registration and Social Security card. You know, stuff I had to have to get financial aid, so I could keep going to college. Some systems are meant to drive men mad, and they work.

I'm not much for sentimental things like pictures, but I will say that I remember everything, and I just need some mental-jogging from time to time. Writing is best done with a hangover, and let's be honest here, drunks always have the best stories to tell.

Chapter 8
Junior Year

So it began much like the year before, except I was working even more hours in Memphis at a fancy hotel on weekends. I had a Tuesday-Thursday class schedule, and, well, being that age and just working nights, I started getting strange requests, and noticing certain females coming in and out at weird hours.

Soon I started getting referral fees for my recommendations. Then other requests came in from younger guests for certain plants and chemicals. I soon made a lot of new friends. After a little while, I had to stop and ask myself, "Why would anybody start doing this type of stuff?"

In the words of the great poets Warren G and Mack 10, "This world is built on material things, but we ain't tripping off that. We want y'all to know this, check it. I want it all: money, fast cars, diamond rings, gold chains, and champagne, shit every damn thing."

So I, like most people brought up in poverty, started slinging. Nothing big, just a dime bag here and a quarter there. I usually just made a phone call here and a phone call there, and a pick up or drop off. I was making $7.50 an hour for like 40 hours a week, and I was bringing in close to $400 in "tips" every weekend. I paid off my car quick. Credit cards were no problem, because I had no need: I carried cash. I started taking my mind off my studies for a while, and then, you know, bars, strip clubs, and some smoke. The rest I was just pissing away.

So I realized my micro and macro professors were idiots, and I started to flunk a few classes. I looked at my roommate Lunch Box, and said, "Bro, I'm tired of this place. I want to transfer to the University of Memphis."

Just like that, we changed over. I got a job on the Tiger High campus, working at the information center in the spring. I also got a raise at the hotel and more hours, mostly because the management was just lazy. I was putting in a good 20+ hours at the information center, giving people directions, meeting all the new girls, other people, making connections on campus, then like 50 or so at the hotel, and 18 hours of classes.

I would hit up the clubs at least five nights a week, after work, before work, or whenever. I was dropping like $250 to $400 a night in bar tabs alone. I felt like I knew everybody, and I did, but none of my family, friends, or co-workers had a clue.

I was working one night in the hotel, and a pimp who made a habit of slapping this one girl around a little too much walked in. I asked why he was doing that shit. He said, "If she don't get paid, I don't get paid, and you don't get paid." He pulled out a gun and pointed it to my head.

I just looked him dead in the eye and said, "Bitch, hold up a second. I got a call coming in."

He said, "What, you calling the cops? Punk, you better."

Then I dropped a name for the first time, who we will call Big Mo.

He said, "How do you know him?! Fuck, never mind, my bad dude. Don't tell him, please, don't." He then emptied out his wallet, and I never saw his face in my hotel again.

Now Big Mo was an old acquaintance that I met a while back, when I was in that mental rehabilitation Hell for a few nights in my early teens. He had rep, and he was helping me out in the supply and demand department for the hotel. But in helping him transition from Mo to Big Mo, I picked up a scar under my right eye, a broken hand, and respect for not taking any shit. Two days after we were last in lockdown together, when I was in middle school, I found out that a prison guard who had been giving us shit had a cousin in my class. After the cousin said some shit to me, I grabbed a pencil and stuck it a good two inches in between his shoulder and neck. He didn't die, but my rep for being crazy grew.

I hadn't seen Big Mo in a long time, but by chance we met up one night at a strip club. Just shooting the breeze while some fat chick was dancing, he noticed my scar, and we started swapping stories of shit that had been going down. He informed me that I didn't owe him shit, and he would provide the goods for me, at cost. I could keep the profits, and if I had any problems, just to give him a ring.

So after the club, we went back to his pad in a part of town white people don't go. Hell, the damn cops wouldn't go there after dark. I met his crew, who said hello with about fourteen AK-47s pointed at me. All of a sudden, they heard the words, "This is my boy. You touch him or his business, you answer to me." Well, two blunts and a bottle of Hennessy later, we had it set up, and we wouldn't meet again unless shit hit the fan. His boys became my errand bitches if I needed them.

Still, everybody who knew me thought I was a guy just going through the motions of life. My grandparents were proud of my grades and happy I was going to the Jewish Student Union. The double life wasn't hard most of the time: I just made phone calls and got money. My GPA was at all-time highs, my wallet would get fat and then slim, spent on concerts, road trips, you name it. Then I got a shock that flipped my world upside down, about a month before my 21st birthday.

Chapter 9
The Death of a Man

So there I was, with spring break approaching, on a Wednesday night out at the local comedy club heckling the redneck on stage. I left in a good mood. I got home and my mother was all, "Sit down."

"Who died?"

"Your father, while on a business trip to Milan, and we're waiting for the consul to call."

I just grabbed the keys, called up Lunch Box, and told him my dad died. We drove around for a time, then went to CK's Coffee Shop and sat there for a while.

I told him, "I'm not sure how to feel. Apparently, it's going to take a while for the body to get shipped back." My dad was coming back to America frozen in a block of ice.

It was very weird for me. I wasn't sure how I was supposed to feel, not sure if I needed to cry or dance. I had mixed emotions, despite the fact I could count on my hands the number of times I actually saw him. I never hated him. I didn't know him well enough for that. I knew he was a funny guy who pulled pranks for kicks. We never really talked.

I mean, my mother had severed that relationship when I was younger. She always forced him into a corner, if we were to talk to him. I remember the time he promised me and my brother that we were going to go to Disneyland. Like kids get, we were super-hyped and jumping up and down in the car. He said we were going in a little while. When a little while took its time arriving, my brother and I put the car in neutral and pushed it out of the garage, and down past about four or five houses. He was so pissed, but he couldn't help but laugh when we finally told him where the car was.

It was one of those "see you when I see you" relationships. I regret it now that I didn't force myself to call more often, but it wasn't my style, or his. I always just reckoned one day we would have a relationship and stuff. I kind of always wanted to live in California but never could pull it off for too long. I remember the time when I was at my cousin's wedding in San Francisco, my dad took me to a lesbian bar after I showed him my fake ID, with my picture and my brother's information on it. He told me he had a lot in common with lesbians, and I found nothing wrong with that.

We joked around for a bit, but it wasn't even like buddy-buddy stuff. We just didn't do that father-son crap. I've known that since I was 5. I don't blame him: if you had to deal with my mother, you would completely understand.

Anyway, after a couple hours, I went to class and imagined pulling the "I know spring break is next week, but my father died in Italy, and I'm not sure when his body will get back, and the funeral is going to be in California, so I'll be gone for a couple of weeks and probably come back with a tan" card to get the grade.

Yeah, that's right: I got sympathy without showing emotion. Now that's the stuff that dreams are made of, kids. My professors heard how screwed up my family was and figured I was normal under those conditions. So I got down to Florida for some fun in the sun, and under the circumstances, I was filled with anticipation and anxiety over all the crap associated with what might come next. My stepmother, mother, brother, aunt, and uncles, everybody was just making it worse.

My brother had a wedding for like 500 people to cater on the weekend of the funeral, so shit got complicated when it came to the funeral planning. It was to be a private ceremony: so would it be ceremony, then burial later, or burial and then ceremony? Were we going to bury him, just to dig him up the next day?

I was going nuts dealing with emotional stuff that I had been trying to shrug off for years. Nobody understood me, and finally I just booked my ticket to California on my own, and my mother started yelling at my aunt to pay for the ticket. What the hell?! Why was I going to be a bargaining chip again, to try to squeeze money out of other people?

So this is the tricky part. I landed at John Wayne Airport, and my cousin picks me up. I had known for years that he smoked the chronic, as they called it back in the day. I had been offered before, but never took it. I had tried the crap I was peddling once or twice and just kind

41

of figured it was all the same. Well, this time, he was like, "No pressure," and I said, "Yeah, I need it." The chronic hit me hard that night, and that was the first time I had used drugs to cope, and it worked.

I got a hold of some valium the next few days and needed every bit of it. The funeral arrangements were such a cluster fuck that my brother, in the end, just said fuck it, and got out of the process. So I was left with being the good son, trying to defend my brother for not coming, when I couldn't, and even to this day don't, forgive him.

I remember dropping a picture of my niece in the grave after the crowd had left. I was an emotional zombie again; it was like lithium minus the drool. I couldn't cry; in fact, I couldn't cry at the fact I couldn't cry, that was saddest part.

Then I had to hear people praise a man I didn't know, and hear about how great of a man he was. I don't know if I was ready for that, yet there I was alone, an outsider.

So upon returning to Memphis, I asked Big Mo for some of the good stuff for me, and that's a mistake when you start hitting your stash. Kids, don't ever get caught up in that circle, you gotta keep 'em separated. I started slipping: while I didn't run into debt while smoking, I was just kind of breaking even. At one point, I started dipping into my own pocket for cash. I took that as a sign to lay off the green, and maybe hitting the bottle just came more naturally. It wasn't a good cycle, but hell, I thought I was having fun.

The rest of my spring was kind of cool. Friends said I was changing; I guess so. I started mixing misery and gin, and like Merle Haggard said, "It looks like you're having a good time, but any fool can see that this honky-tonk heaven makes you feel like Hell," or something like that. I coasted the rest of that semester and the summer semester.

I was just wasted, but on the outside I was doing great, with a 3.5 GPA. I couldn't pass the required foreign languages or Re-Construction history, due to my anti-federalist stance on the Constitution. So I found a loophole: if I took public affairs, I wouldn't have to deal with the depressing facts about the aftermath of the War of Northern Aggression.

I played little games during class with the big words on the board and, come the midterm, I had a few too many gin and tonics. I got to writing my essay, and the professor called me out, asking if I had been drinking. I said that I had one or two, and he grabbed my essay and started grading it, nodding his head.

Then I left, showed up next class, and he said, "Unfortunately, somebody was listening in class and screwed up the curve for everybody else." He told me, had I not had one or two drinks, I might not have had five or six misspelled words, and that's why I only got a 97. To top it off, he gave me the option of not coming to class or taking any more tests.

I couldn't help it, I enjoyed his rants on worthless bureaucrats, and all I did was question anybody thinking they knew better than me. Who the hell are they to tell me what's right or wrong? They don't know me, I'm just a Mother Fucking Survivalist™, doing what I got to do to get by, and I'm doing it my way!

I spent my free time shooting pool, beers, and espresso, sleeping two hours at a time at most. Moonshine for some events, and the chronic for every movie I saw, just trying to find a hero or a role-model. I would be remiss not to mention some women, but, look, I figured out a long time ago, women dig dudes who treat them like shit, so starting shit in bars by grabbing chicks' asses and then buying them shots seemed to work for me. I worked at a hotel, and I had keys to an office on campus with a couch. Respect!

Chapter 10
9/11 and the Internship

So look, there I am again, sobering up for the next semester, laying off the stuff I was selling because of some crackdowns. Then I changed my major again, because I still couldn't grasp the foreign language thing: I'm an American, they speak English everywhere else I wanted to go. I never stopped to look back when I got into political science, because I realized I was good at making shit up on the fly, all silver-tongued.

So I took constitutional law, and with my previous class in Media Law, I kind of had the jargon down well enough to fake my way to the top of the class early on. It was at night; Lunch Box was in the class with me. It was cool: we would debate shit after class and look up obscure ways to beat the system. I played my word games in the class, and while the professor was speaking, I looked busy as hell writing stuff down, because I would just take a big word, like legislative intent, and try to make as many words as I could out of it, like tit, tent, cunt, and just go down the list, making a big list, seeing how many words I could make in the hour and half class. I looked busy as hell! Some other people caught on to what I was doing and tried it for a while, to no avail, for they lacked the mad skills I had. I was grooving through the class and decided that maybe I should be a lawyer or something.

9/11 happened and immediately I thought, why are they freaking out? Didn't people watch G.I. Joe or ever read about the Muslim fundamentalists in Afghanistan? These assholes were passing new asshole laws and doing crazy stuff, like blowing up huge Buddhas carved into mountain sides. Not to mention making non-Muslims wear gold stars, that kind of hit home. These crazy fuckers called themselves the Taliban, and right after that, I knew they were going to be looking for terrorists, and that meant fucking wiretapping.

I started reading about the PATRIOT law and wrote a term paper on it. Funny, when I was doing the term paper, it was hard as all hell to find any real sources on the law. I found an obscure column and used it as a guide to rant and rave.

I also called off the funny business I was doing for a little bit. It cut my cash flow, but I had picked up another job doing promotions for a large cigarette company, that hired another company, to hire us to promote the smoking experience. We went into bars, signed people up, and they got cool stuff. I found myself back in the bars and clubs I was hanging out at anyways, three or four nights a week, and they paid like $14 an hour. Hanging out until 5 or 6 in the morning, same people every night almost, just different places. It was cool, because I got to card chicks and get their phone numbers. One night I got a hold of some E and was working the floor, so I picked up one chick after the next and just snuck into the van or a bathroom.

That was cool, and my bosses thought I was doing great work. It was work and good, legit work, too. I mostly just talked to people all night, and then hit the afterhours bars and clubs, which became my new hangouts, and they were cheaper. I partook of the occasional reefer action, but not for escaping purposes, more for chillin' and partying purposes.

Along the way, I saw these signs for a Tennessee State Legislature Internship program. It required a minimum 3.0 GPA and stuff. At the time, my overall GPA was still like 2.6. My general education classes blew, and the program had other requirements way out of my league. I was doing just fine coasting along, and my professor told me, "I think you should do the internship."

I said, "I don't meet the requirements," and he said to just find some recommendation letters from professors in this department. The only other prof I had was the crazy guy, but okay, I'll do some brown-nosing. If I get turned down, I have a better chance at playing the "aw-shucks" face for a good grade on my final.

Well, they called me in to interview, and I just told the lady that I don't know anything about government, except it doesn't work that well. She said that was okay, just write an essay. So I wrote the "I'm just a poor boy looking for truth and trying to provide for my family" essay. I did like 15 pages in 45 minutes. I was having fun with the whole thing.

I got accepted. Hell, I had no idea what I was going to be doing or for who. I focused on all my grades, closed up shop, quit the hotel, quit the info center, and the promo stuff. I had to take a big pay cut, so I asked for a small loan from Big Mo, who said, "Talk to my boy when you get there."

So I got up to Nashville, and I'm sitting through all this crap about security, sexual harassment in the work place, and other stuff about trying to be professional. I was looking around the room, bored, knowing I shouldn't be there. Then I met this cat named Kongo, who asked if I smoked. And I was like, "Smoke what?" I hadn't picked up cigarettes yet, and we held a meeting of the minds over lunch and met later. We eventually made one bowl worth of resin last three months. Top that.

I didn't have any money yet, but I figured I would yell at Big Mo's boy. So I called the hotel number I got, and was like, "Yeah, Big Mo told me to give you a shout."

Dude on the other end was like, "Are you white?! I don't do that shit. Man, you a cop?"

I was like, "No, damn it, dude, I'm just looking for some green."

He asked me what I did, so I told him. The next day we got our assignments, namely which state representatives and senators we would be working for. I got the hippie holdover from the late 60s, the Iron Colonel, and also another guy whose first words to me were, "You're not as cute as our last intern. Go talk to Debbie."

So anyway, somehow I got sent to get supplies, and I was just wandering the halls, and hopped in an elevator. I heard the words, "Hold that elevator, cracker," so I did. Then I looked the guy over some: he was well known, and I recognized the voice. If you're from Memphis, I know you've seen him in the paper.

"So, you goin' to be working for me some."

I was all like, "No man, I got these two dudes," and then he pulled out a wad of cash and stuffed it in my pocket. Then he said, "No, you working for me. Keep yo' eyes open round here, learn something while you here, boy. Don't go calling me no more, and better not call Mo. Stay away from that other green, and I'll take care of you, boy."

Since I was the first one in the office and because I lived across the street (and I'm fly like that), I got to deliver the morning papers to the Democrats on my way in and to make the coffee. Other than that, I ran to the mail room, grabbed some coffee, and walked the halls when nothing was going on. I got a reputation for being quick to get out of doing any real work; I suppose people thought I was busy, or maybe they knew I didn't belong. Whatever.

After three days, I figured the building out and realized to Hell with getting my good suits out and dry cleaning for this stuff! I would throw on the maroon blazer and a thin knit tie. I went all retro on them, but it was a cheaper dry cleaning bill, and I guess I had a budget to live on.

My first weekend there I parked the Shalom Stallion (my red Camaro) out behind the building and started walking to the downtown bars, and stumbling down Printers Alley at three or four in the morning. I passed by some strip clubs and what not. I had my eyes and wallet open. After dropping the extra cash I had in two or three nights, I met a blonde who came in town a couple of nights a week and wanted a place to crash. Two weeks later, she started spilling me some dirt on the people I worked with. I started to let it be known that I frequented all the bars on any given night of the week, and I might shake your hand. I also let a nod in ye old elevator suffice for "Gotcha!"

Pretty soon, I knew who was cool and who wasn't. I knew the lobbyist parties had free alcohol, but it was more fun talking to elected officials at three in the morning, when they were all liquored up and hitting on some young piece. I also went back to my "master", with a note in a committee meeting, or in the back halls used for smoking in the building. After a short while, the blonde was a regular in my studio apartment, so I upgraded from air mattress to futon.

Anyways, I hung out with Kongo, walked the halls nodding at random people, and pretty soon they just assumed I caught them out the night before. I went out for lunch with the "master". When it came to watching the legislators go at it, the committee meetings were okay, but caucus meetings were the best. Once again, it was like I was living a separate life, hanging out with Kongo until late, then walking back to my pad and peeking around corners to see who was where.

I would give a note and a nod, and the vote would come out a certain way in committee, and I had money to maintain my lifestyle. Big bar tabs and lap dances weren't cheap, but I got to meet a lot of nice grad students who went to Vanderbilt. I began riding back and forth to Memphis with Kongo, who it turns out went to Memphis State also.

I went back to get some cash for my good work. Every now and then, at a certain club around six or seven on Sunday mornings, I would catch Big Mo and my "master", and we would have some pancakes. In the halls, it was all business for me, kind of: I would bend the rules on harassment, not always sexual, just plain harassing. A girl named "Drapes" worked in the same office, and being that she had actual work to do and I didn't, I would just sit and poke her in the side with my pencil, just for shits and giggles.

I had two phones, and I loved drunk-dialing, so I made a few enemies in the halls. Kongo had an amazing video game collection, so hanging with him on an almost nightly basis was a given. We also had "Fun with Doug Night", and I'll explain why. Doug was this dweeb, cripple, retard who was also interning with us, and he was all Christian-conservative, but with a mustache that would make a 70s porn star jealous.

So Kongo and I had a habit of hanging out with Doug, usually Tuesday nights, but we soon discovered "Fun With Doug Night" was way more fun without Doug there! So we subbed in Scott, or Buster, and maybe Little Buddy. We watched a lot of Three Amigos and rocked out, but not with our cocks out: this was a bunch of guys having a good time, not a gay orgy.

Wandering amongst the filth in the halls of the State Legislature, I learned how political deals were done, even got a few things done the way I wanted. Of course, my coworkers who did real work (instead of just pretending to be reading War and Peace) were jealous. I took notes and started office files that I got to name: "Speed Humps", "Cripples Can't Dance", "You Can't Hang With Mr. Cooper", and whatnot. Let's face it, they got references, I got satisfaction. They went to law school or whatever, I lived the life.

Around that time, peer pressure from the Fire Demon (you'd understand if you met her) got me to take the LSAT. I took one pretest, and she's still pissed that I didn't study and almost maxed out the test. She scored embarrassingly low, but she is a lawyer now.

Anyways, I soon realized how corrupt the system was, but either way, I was doing good. I held a night of drinking to honor my father's death during the internship. I told everybody that I wasn't coming in for work the next day, so I called in drunk ahead of time. So when I missed a day, my secretary Debbie was convinced that I was face-first in a gutter. Which I was for a good part of the evening, before I made it home.

I learned just how much I could drink in a night, and how much I had to drink the next day to properly come down from a night of binge drinking. I have never puked alcohol, or from the effects of alcohol. Now coffee the next morning, that shit happens sometimes. I have blacked out and woken up in other states. I can hold my liquor even when I should have had my stomach pumped. So Debbie got three state reps to force Kongo to come over and check on me, even though he told her I was fine. Sometimes a man just needs to drink.

Look, I'm guessing I spent close to $1,200 on my own tab at three bars and two houses that night. The next day, I hit the bars at noon, with another $500 spent by closing time. Well, look, you can't win 'em all. I was just trying to come down slow, to avoid the shakes.

At the mock legislative session our class did, I mocked the mock and protested. I got kicked out of the session for refusing to yield the floor, when I was busy decrying the evils committed by the state of Mississippi, in collusion with France, that were "too heinous to be mentioned here." If that shit ever comes back to bite the world in the ass, don't say you weren't warned, because you were. You know damn well what I'm talking about!

So even though I got wrestled out of the Tennessee House by some East Tennessee Nazi Mountain Gorillas, that doesn't mean you don't fight 'em back! Never back down, but don't start any shit, won't be none.

So the internship was all good until my last week. I had packed up, because the school was no longer paying me, and my "master" thought it would be funny for me to drive his car back for him to Memphis. When I got pulled over in his vehicle, and the trooper demanded I open the trunk, I realized just how deep I was. I didn't go along with it, because I knew the trooper didn't have anything on me and couldn't make me.

But when I got back, I checked it out for myself. As I looked inside, I noticed some rather large packages of something wrapped in foil and then sealed. When I got back and gave him his keys, he said, "Thank you for not offending my honor by saying my name. If you ever offended my honor, I would be forced to challenge you to a duel. I got more money than you, and I can always get more guns."

Chapter 11
The Road To Graduation

I continued to work for people during the summer and for the fall elections, but I had started working on campus as Parking Nazi. My job was writing tickets, but mainly just being cool, riding around campus on a golf cart. I pimped a position that most people were like, "How can you pimp that?" I told them, "You gotta play your hand as the cards are dealt."

I'd been all in for a while, working the system like a modern day Robin Hood. I used my authority to pick up chicks and to get in close with the campus police. I didn't appear to be much, riding around with a boom box bumping and zinc oxide on my nose, chilling on a golf cart. I had the system working for me: I had a gate key that got me into any parking lot I chose, people knew not to ticket my car, and the cops didn't harass me for speeding around campus.

I wrote close to 400 tickets on a day when I needed to prove a point to one of the full-time ticket writers, namely that a barely literate monkey could do a better job than them. Most other times, I would just drive around, open gates that were broken, collect the meters, fix the meters, and ride the campus in a manner that made even the adjunct faculty feel that I had somehow sparked a revolution of one, slacking against all odds and all gods of campus life.

I took the job for women, beer, and gas, and I did it better than anyone else. When it came to taking perks, it was nothing big, aside from phone numbers, or the guy seeing me out later that night buying me a beer for just giving him a warning ticket. I wasn't selling on campus, but I acted like I was a gorilla pimp, working every angle, getting rid of tickets for my own professors, in exchange for a blind eye here and a blind eye there.

My only real concern was about the letter I received, claiming I owed $85,000 in back child support. Yeah, that's right, my father died, and then I received the bill for money that should have been paid to me during my childhood. I had to go tell a judge in California that I don't

51

owe myself 85 grand in child support, and then they dropped it. But still, that's how shit goes in my world.

I had an ethics class that made my life easy, not because I knew anything about ethics, but because I was able use my shock and awe technique my first day, lowering the bar for success. Going around the room that day, I was asked what I was going to do upon graduation. I informed the class of my goal: to open a pirate radio station off the east coastline, and then raise an army and conquer half the known world. Later in that ethics class, we had to team up with somebody and draw an assignment of a situational thing, and do kind of a "live on the scene reporting" skit, and explain the ethical questions to follow.

I reenacted the incident at Columbine High School, in a trench coat with stink bombs and string guns. I went all out, with Captain Kirk rolls and high fives, and just making a mockery of the whole thing. My partner thought it was funny and was doing her reporting thing. Afterwards, I got an A for my reenactment, and I was informed it was hands-down the best presentation he had ever witnessed in 30+ years of teaching. That professor became my advisor and chairman of my thesis review panel.

I got asked to go to work at a bankrupt hotel, as a part time night auditor and afternoon desk worker. I did, and soon the girls and guys began to leave the old hotel and started staying at my new hotel. The tips started coming in, from pizza to beer, and of course, hard currency. Someone came in to rob me one night; I just looked at him, and he said, "Shit, it's you! Please don't tell anyone! I didn't know you were protected." He left, and I got a call from Big Mo at the hotel, apologizing for the misunderstanding, and asking me to stop by after work on my way to school.

Well, I got to the meeting spot, and the dude was hog-tied, and my "master" and Big Mo were there. Big Mo asked me if that was the guy who tried to rob me, and I said yes. And I heard a boom, as his knee cap had just been blown out with a 12-gauge shot gun. Then a gun was placed at his head, and, "click", the guy pissed his pants. The gun was empty, but he didn't know that.

He offered to do anything, and that was how I got in over my head. A duffel bag was buried right there on the spot, and inside was 100 grand, the gun, and I was informed that nobody comes here to dig it up; it remains there. My "master" spoke and said that 100 grand was just money, and that this had to do with business. It was a small price to pay for me to keep all the revenue from my business, and he knew I wasn't a rat. But he didn't trust that guy in the ground; he said robbing me was like a slap in his face.

Then I got a security guard at the hotel who was on two payrolls. I began working for some local politicians, helping distribute flyers door to door. So I took bad areas, sent three girls into the neighborhoods, and made a call informing the right people that they were not to be touched. It wasn't big money: I got paid 20 cents a flyer, and I paid the girls 10 cents per flyer that got on people's door steps.

Back at school, I no longer cared. I would make the occasional trip to Missouri, delivering packages to a farm and to buy some lottery tickets. I was still low-profile, until I received a subpoena to appear before a federal grand jury. I went to a lawyer's house, and at the time it was close to midnight. He laughed at me for running over, and said, "Why didn't you call my office?"

"Subpoena," I said. "Look at the name they are going to question me about."

He said, "Shit, what do you want to do?"

I said, "I want no record of my name, and no real testimony. I'll answer their questions, but nothing other than a statement will they get."

It just became real for me. The lawyer said he would do it for free, and he arranged for me to give a deposition with no name attached. I answered questions regarding a Rolex, to the tune of, "Yeah, lots of people have nice watches. I don't wear a watch, 'cause time isn't a priority to me."

They said, "Did you ever hear how this man got his watch?"

I replied with, "Money, I guess. It never crossed my mind to ask him where he got it. I personally wouldn't ask you where you got your tie at."

Much of the deposition was crap, but after four hours, they were still nowhere and hadn't asked me any questions towards anything else illegal I had done, or that I knew other people had done. Then I saw a picture of me, Mo, and my "master" in a field, watching a hole being filled. The suckers had shown up, just an hour too late.

The investigator asked me, "What were you doing there with those men?"

At this point my lawyer said, "It's time to go. This was a witch hunt. This wasn't part of your question list, nor does it have anything to do with my client."

I was out the door and on my way home, and I got pulled over by some flashing lights. The guy asked me to step out of the car. He handed me a phone, and I heard a voice say, "You did good today, nice job refusing to crack. You need to slow down your non-legal practices for a while, maybe even take a vacation in the spring."

That was all. I got back in my car and hit the bar. I was back on the bar scene again whenever I was off work, to the point the bartenders asked me to barback on Wednesday nights. Just go grab empty pitchers and bring them to the bar. So, I had found another job.

I was working close to 85 hours a week total, including a weekend schedule that looked like this: 8-10 Parking Nazi, school 10-1, Parking Nazi 1-7, bar 7-9, hotel 11-7, parking office 7:30 to 2, hotel 11-7, and hotel 3-11. Come Monday, I was dead on my feet in class and in the parking office. I normally found a spot in the afternoon to catch a quick nap.

This semester was killing me, having to defend my graduation plan to a board, including the pirate radio station idea. Now, I did this very well, pointing out that the station would be in international waters broadcasting on a frequency that was not being used. I also agreed to do a final project with the thesis, a voter registration campaign. That wasn't due until May, and I was still running the campus like I owned the place.

I met an old acquaintance from high school, and we began hanging out during my free time, smoking, drinking, and hustling pool for some cash on the side. It felt like I was in the movie "Dazed and Confused".

I would still go by my grandparents' house in my free time, checking up on my grandmother, who had dementia. She kept making me promise to never marry a New Yorker, because she didn't want me to make the same mistake she did. My grandfather was normally asleep on the recliner, watching some Western, and she was just kind of stuck, not even being able to remember how to work the remote. I always enjoyed her company. She made me wish I was just a little more than I was. I always wanted to do good for her, so she could rub it in other people's faces.

Eventually, I got tired of the rat-race, somewhere in the working hard phase, and just wanted to be left alone to smoke some pot. I was forced to change my suppliers because of the heat around town. I was still being followed for a good part of my day, and that spot with the money was still being watched. I passed it every day on my way to school and work. I often debate going and digging it up now, but I tend to chicken out, for fear of the feds.

So there I am, doing what I got to do to keep up with everything, and it hits me: life is hard, and I'm getting tired of all the bullshit. Me and Mr. Funktastic were smoking up a storm, and Kongo and his new girl were getting pretty serious. It was a Thursday night a little after Thanksgiving, and I had just gotten my LSAT scores back. I got a 169 out of 180, and it was good enough to get accepted into every school that I could ever dream of applying to. Only my other grades were going to pull me down, and I knew law school was the fastest way to a heart attack. That's why I never went: I didn't want the stress it would bring, no matter how much it paid.

I was barbacking one night, and I went outside for a drink, and then it all went black. I came to later, with my pants ripped, my head hurting, and my ankle felt bad. I had just been run over by a car, and I had the tread marks on my pants and shirt to prove it. It took me a few days to realize that I was invincible: a car can't kill me, so I sure as Hell ain't going to live my life the way others want me to!

This was my moment of clarity, my Zen if you will. I could do whatever I wanted to. I was above reproach by other men, because I should have been dead at that point. When you take a car on and can still talk afterwards, get back to me.

I took some time off from the hotel, and that's when the dingbat mother of mine decided to go to the hotel I worked at and try to get my job. Lucky for me, the manager liked me, so he didn't hire her. Somewhere around this time, my mother answered a call on the house phone. It was a girl, and my mother essentially interrogated her, and somehow made the girl feel like a whore for asking to borrow my notes. This changed my feelings about the situation I was working on with the girl, because I couldn't show my face around her after that. In class or at work, I just felt well embarrassed.

I felt cheapened; my mother had just slapped my pride. My pride said, "Fuck you, bitch!", and me and Mr. Funktastic grabbed all the drugs, liquor, cash and cigarettes we could find and hit the road. I dropped all the classes I didn't need to graduate and called my thesis and project advisors to advise them I would do the work from the road. Thus began the great trek to find my future and towards getting the hell out of Dodge.

So away we went, in search of all that adventure people read about, or think about, but never do. We burnt all of our bridges and hit the gas pedal, just going for it, not wondering what we were going to do or how, just by the seat of our pants. After switching shifts driving the first night, me and Mr. Funktastic pulled off to a camp ground, and there we hit the bottle hard, took way too many pills, and smoked a joint.

Next thing I knew, we were surrounded by snow somewhere in Oklahoma. We decided to go north, and I placed a call to my uncle, telling him, "Me and a buddy are on a road trip. If we get to Denver, I'll give you call." We got there just before New Year's, and we hung out at a friend from high school's place for a while.

We mainly just chilled out in Denver. My uncle was cool and offered to get us a little work. We wound up painting some apartments for a slum lord in the ghetto, but we got to crash there at night. It was great, when my uncle got a call from Mr. Funktastic's dad, who had the title to the car. This made things complicated, to put it mildly. At this point, my uncle offered to send me to Europe for a few months, all expenses paid. As he did for my other cousins at one point or another, he felt like it would be a chance to see the world and figure out what I wanted to do. I told him that I couldn't just leave my friend hanging like that.

By now, we had started to get more and more into smoking and drinking ourselves stupid. After a while, he hooked up with a dog trainer, and I found my way into a spot with two lesbians, who offered me a place to sleep and some cash in exchange for helping them have a kid. I hate to sound like a man-whore, but, well, it made sense at the time, as far as I was concerned. It was a great deal for me!

Then my uncle informed me that he had to go to LA to help out a friend, and he suggested that we leave the car behind. He would give us a ride to Vegas, and my cousin offered to pick us up in Vegas. We could take a trip through Death Valley and go skiing in the Sierra Nevadas. I didn't say no.

It was a nice change, but it didn't take long for everybody to get on each other's nerves, but we made the most of it. Staying in Vegas, we picked up some chicks at a local bar and then made do. We were having a blast, and we made our way to Death Valley with my cousin. We found this camping spot with a homemade spring, which had made some vegetation growing in it, in the hottest place in America I had ever been.

It was there, while smoking, that I felt the souls of the Native Americans that had been there before us. It felt as if I had just eaten the lives of those who had come before me. I felt spiritual for the first time in life. How? Why? Not sure, but it felt good.

We then headed for the mountains, as my cousin had some friends who lived there. It was there I learned to ski using the "snow plow and duck walk" method. After a day and a half on the kiddy slopes, one of my cousin's friends got me up on the double black diamond run. I attacked it head-on and made my way straight down the mountain, wind flying in my face. I felt like a million bucks! I was living life on the edge.

Towards the end of the run, I saw the group at the bottom, and knew there weren't no way I was gonna stop, so I just laid back and let the mountain take me. I did two back flips and slid down a little, but, man, did that feel like freedom. My cousin started laying into me about safety, and about me not having insurance, and what if this, what if that. Kind of a bummer for me, but I had a ball. I didn't care.

We proceeded to make our way to the Bay area, and for a while it was all gravy. We were crashing at my aunt and uncle's. I discovered that I had some issues with my teeth, which needed a whole lot of dental treatment done. My uncle, who was a dentist, was doing a good three hours a day working on my teeth, and then me and Mr. Funktastic would do some work for my aunt or my cousin.

We managed to get a hold of some mushrooms, and that's when the world became an interesting place. There were so many colors, and then the paranoia hit me, and I came to the conclusion that if nothing else went right ever again, I could always just go into some sort of mental facility. We managed to get into the liquor cabinet a bit too much. We then made a trip down to LA, to visit my cousin's girlfriend's cousin, who was a hair dresser.

It was all good, but I'll get back to a better LA story later. Driving up to the ocean on shrooms is one of those things everybody should do, as it was one of those views that words can't describe. Even then, the only thing I could come up with to describe its beauty was the fact that the ocean was just The Ocean, so big and beautiful. It was one of those things that just had a lasting impact on me.

So anyways, back to the game. I managed to get most of my graduation work done at or around Berkley, getting surveys and general information from random people on the street. My professor in charge of statistics loved the Berkley thing. Even more, he thought what I was doing was great, and he said to just see him when I got back.

We were still doing stuff, keeping busy, and still rock and rolling through the States. We finally got up north to Seattle. Sitting on the Grey Hound, about every 15 minutes it would stop, so we would hop off, smoke a quick bowl, and get back on. I was packing in the dark and ready every time we stopped. We met some other folks with the same plan of attack.

We finally arrive in Seattle, and I gave my brother a call, so we stayed at his in-laws' house. We did some minor work, met one of my brother's employees who DJ'ed on the side, and we went with him to a club to meet his girlfriend and her friends. We hung out with them; they were cool, and it made Seattle interesting.

Graduation day was coming closer and closer, and I was still polishing my paper work. Fudging some stats my way, if you know what I mean. It became apparent that in order to graduate, I would need to come back to Memphis and work with a few professors. Graduation was about two weeks away, so my grandmother bought me a ticket back.

I returned home, leaving Mr. Funktastic behind. I meant to return and finish what I had started, but it just never worked out that way. I realized making plans isn't really my strong point. Anyways, I stayed up all night, finished the written part and got my stats approved. However, I needed to do a voter registration campaign, so I made a power point, did some radio spots over the computer mic, and borrowed a video camera from Kongo. We did some really rough spots that were all one take and done.

While me and Kongo were walking around Confederate Park along the river looking for a spot to do some more shooting, we met this guy named Lawyer. Yeah, he was homeless, and I asked him if he would speak on the importance of voting to the younger generation. I offered him a 40 oz. and some cigarettes for his help. It was by far the best part of my campaign. Hell, we cut the camera off after a good 15 minutes, and he spoke for another 30.

As I was on a deadline putting everything together, I found this effect on power point that would give a round of applause after each screen. I did it to stay awake; I figured I would keep it on until I was done with the last one, and then take it off. I guessed wrong: no matter how I tried to take it off, it just wouldn't stop. I got a little tired of screwing with thing and just said, "Fuck, I'll leave it be."

I finished it all two days before grades were due in, and less than a week until I WOULD WALK. Now getting to my advisor, who was avoiding me like the plague, was a bitch. I talked to his grad assistant for a good week, and finished copy in hand, I sat in front of his office for two days waiting to give it to him. I went home thinking, "Oh well," and then I got a call from his assistant: she said I had five minutes to get there.

I got there in three, parked on the grass behind the back door of the building, and ran up the back stairwell. Look who I see sneaking out the back door, my advisor, who needed to sign off on my project! He asked, "How do you think you did on it?"

I told him, "Probably a B."

He said, "I think it takes balls to catch me leaving and admit it's a B. I'll give you an A, and we will call it a day. Have a nice life."

Just like that, I was done with college. I went to my old bar hangout, and some folks bought me some beers, and then I went to a party across the way at another fraternity house. I met some chick who caught me gazing into the vast nothingness in the sky. It was then and there that I found the perfect pick-up line.

She asked me what I was doing, and I replied, "Just wondering what else there is. It's so big and beautiful out there. You know, I haven't missed a sunrise or a sunset in the past six months. I find it comforting, the fact that the sky keeps changing. It helps me do some soul-searching and self-reflection."

"Why do you need to do self-reflecting?" I was asked.

I answered, "Because I'm not perfect, nor do I pretend to be, but I think there is room for me to grow and become a better me."

This line was all truth, and it was also the quickest I had ever picked up a girl. When I woke up before sunrise, I took her with me to a spot to watch the sun come up. All she could do was thank me for showing her the power of the heavens above. Honestly, I was just speaking the truth, but it made me question everything.

I wound up graduating and debating what to do with my newfound life style, that of a hippie, I suppose. I got a job delivering Chinese food three hours a day. I was thrilled, but I knew I was missing something, and quoting the good chairman Mao wasn't helping. I began using this vibe I had picked up, which was that of someone questioning everything, looking for a deeper meaning in life.

All the while, my mother was driving me crazy about this and that; I wanted her to get her own life. Anyways, my grandfather gave me his old car as a graduation present, and I began looking for work, but the Chinese food thing was doing ok in my book: about $15 a day in tips, and I got to take home a plate from the buffet.

Chapter 12
First Jobs

So I kept up the Chinese thing, doing some hemp jewelry on the side as well, nothing but wasting time and searching for a better way of life. I avoided doing stuff illegal, except for the occasional drug use and what not. The hotel where the Chinese food restaurant was happened to be the hotel I used to work at. They were finally about to be sold, and all the people there began to worry about their jobs.

They soon realized that new management wasn't going to hire them. My mother was already inside with the new owners group, and after delivering food one day, I got summoned to an interview they were having. I was wearing an old tie-dyed t-shirt full of holes, shorts, and some flip flops. When I went in, I threw my feet on the meeting table, leaned back, and said, "How much are you going to pay me?" Their jaws dropped.

I corrected myself before anybody else said anything. "I want $13 an hour."

The head guy said, "Why would we pay you that?"

I informed him that I knew the computer system, including the general manager's password, just in case the current workers got wind that their services won't be needed. Oh, and I would also need a room there. They asked me if I could train everybody, work the night shift, and would I take $9.50 an hour?

I realized I would be getting overtime and agreed to $10.25 an hour, on the conditions they kept Grimace, my favorite security guard, I got a room on property, and I could leave after everyone was trained. Well, I got it. I started having to train everybody and do the night audit, and soon I was going crazy. The house I had been living in for the past seven years or so was under renovations, as Lunch Box's dad was doing the work, and he spent most of the time asleep. Which meant the hotel was my new home.

I worked hard, smoked when I could, but mainly just worked, getting phone calls every two hours with stupid shit, like, "I'm short 15 cents, what do I do?!" I had to do my drinking on nights that I had off, but that was rarely happening, so I would grab a few while working overnight. Red Bull and vodka became a life line for me.

You might say, "How dare he drink on the job, or get high! That's bad business!" I was never late, my money was always spot on, and mistakes were non-existent on my shifts. No, we had some stupid people working there, including my mother, but I only had to show her a couple of times. The two Mexicants (I know how I spelled it; it's the more correct way to describe their people) were driving me crazy with stupid, petty garbage like, "How do I charge a credit card?" or "I put the wrong rate in the computer."

I told them to make a note, I'll fix it later, but that was apparently impossible for them to understand. So I had to go clock-in, fix the issue in a couple of minutes, but, hell, I'm up now, so I made them practice this crap, so I didn't have to do this again.

It was around this time I quit getting regular haircuts and shaving. My regulars loved the fact I was doing hemp work on the side and would often buy random stuff from me, because they thought it was cool. People around here just didn't do that type of stuff anymore. Well I was, and I picked up some chicks who were passing through town, because my pickup line was the golden ticket.

I did work hard, and I did play hard, but I also was trying to do right: avoid gang life and gang members. This was something I found easier the more and more I started hating money, and the things people would do for it. The girls that worked the afternoon shift were cool: I grew up with one, and the other was cool. I did my best to get people to stay there, but renovations were coming, and management wasn't exactly the sharpest tools in the shed. They were morons.

The time came for me to leave, so I gave my two week notice, then applied for a job as a pizza cook and got the job as a manager. Now this sounded good to me: the pay sucked, but free food and the occasional beer was nice. I made some money at a casino: it wasn't enough, it never is when it comes to money. It turns out I went to high school with one of the guys I was working with, and we did some grass during our safety meetings. When we got off work, it was like, "Let's hit up a club and get stoned!"

So yes, this was my life: working to get stoned, and that led to just getting stoned whenever I could. I had a new connection, and my old connection was giving my new connection some issues. Then I made a phone call from work and got a large shipment in. Me and my friend were going to sell what we could, but wound up at his place most nights smoking, and the girls we met all just wanted our drugs. It was funny: here I am, acting like a drug lord, or at least like a 70s porn star.

I didn't let anybody go easy, and often would have problems making my money back, but the discount was good, and the new go-between guy was perfect. Monday was pay day, and Tuesday the girl with the prescription pad would come by and sell us scripts. By Thursday, we were always broke, needing tips for smokes, and of course, we always had extra weed to sell. It became a running joke, us bartering weed and pizza for women, beer, and cigarettes.

I was doing the best I could to keep it all together working overtime, but to be honest with you, I felt empty, and the only way for me to fill the void I felt was to keep busy and to look for more meaning. Doing drugs seemed logical, and then it happened one day. Minda (my mother) had done my laundry, found a large package of green stuff, and confronted me in front of Lunch Box. I told her I had no clue what that was and to let me see it. She threw it at me, and I said, "Oh yeah, that's just oregano."

She called me out, but whatever, bitch was driving me crazy. In between work and play, my sleeping at home was rare, but it happened. So anyways, I had to let the weed dry out. I told my coworkers about it, and we all had a big laugh. A few days later, I smelled the stuff, and it had improved in quality by smell, and when I smoked it, it was like Heaven. It burned nice and slow, had good flavor and an aroma to satisfy. I sold the rest of it to clear enough money to cover another batch.

Around this time, I was getting bored with life. I thought about killing myself, but never got around to it. I stuck with driving fast while drunk, doing excessive amounts of pills, and snorting heroin whenever the opportunity arose. The stuff didn't fill the void, and I hated life even more, working 50-60 hours a week, the same people everywhere I went. I couldn't take it.

I would go over to my friend's girlfriend's house after work to smoke, and then go play some pool. We made brownies a couple times, and, yes, I was also taking a Fashion Merchandising class. Since I was the only dude in the class, the girls thought maybe I was gay. But after a week, they realized I was straight, but just happened to know my shit when it came to fashion. I managed to win over a few girls in the class and was doing well, but the drugs were taking over.

I couldn't escape the idea that life was just not worth all this crap, and I kept trying to make life better, but kept sinking further and further under. Now I was having a blast on the outside. I would get behind with my connection and tell him to call Big Mo, and then my connection would bring me cash the next time I saw him.

That cash would normally get blown in the strip clubs, the only place I really felt comfortable. These places were like brothels or something, but there was truth in the clubs. Something about naked women selling their bodies for cash made more sense than to go out on a date and pretending not to have sex on my mind.

Around this time, me and the blonde from Nashville started back up again. I would crash at her place, or at the very least, hang out before going home to my worthless existence. I suppose me and the blonde had a good thing going, so one day I proposed to her with a hemp ring. It was all good for a while; I figured this was how life worked.

Then one day, I walked in on her and another girl, and she said it was a present. Sex with two girls became the norm, I guess. After a while, it became three or four girls at a time. Something was missing, and when I tried to break it off, she flipped her shit.

I eventually just went crazy. I got a passport and was debating how bad life was. One of the girls turned out to be connected to a police officer, and she threatened me not to do anything I would regret. I figured, crap, how much worse can it get? It didn't matter; other people thought I was happy, so I must be happy!

Oh boy, I was just asking for trouble, day in and day out. I started making my goal in life to catch up to Wilt Chamberlain, who claimed to have slept with over 10,000 women. It seemed like a worthy mission in life; life was still empty, but at least I had a goal.

With my hair long and my beard thick, people would double take and ask me if I was Jesus. Why I don't know, it just kind of happened. People are stupid. I appeared to give off the vibe, and I didn't care much for others. Hell, I hardly cared about myself. All I wanted was some sort of signal, some type of reason for the madness.

One day, I started thinking back on my life, and how things could have been. Well, when you wake up, your back hurts, and you have a bunch of doped-up strippers surrounding you, then you can question me; until then, shut up and read. I got up and decided that maybe I should have been more religious, like my brother: he seemed happy.

Then I started asking questions, asking myself, "What kind of world do you want to live in?" None of this mattered; my real problem was that I was living with five chicks, and one was a cop. So I did what made sense: I videotaped her and two other girls.

Later, I went by to see Big Mo, told him the problem, and gave him the tape, should I ever need another copy. Mo wrote an address down and told me to give it to her. I gave her the note, and the next day she had arrested five dealers. Then she thanked me and gave me a number to call, should I ever get harassed again. She follows that up with telling me she is now in the organized crime unit, and in exchange for some cash, would Mo and I pass info on people from another organization?

Everybody was happy with the arrangement except me. When I finally looked in the mirror and realized all I had were these girls, who were constantly fighting over money and drugs. I told the blonde with my hemp ring on that this was it. She was pissed, but didn't fight it. She understood I was going full throttle into everything, and I wasn't going to be looking back anytime soon.

I was partying like a rock star before it was cool. I had a life filled with sex, drugs, and rock and roll, but inside I had nothing left to give. About this time, I decided to get the passport and put it to use. I sat back at Starbucks and tried to figure out what to do next. Mo met me in public, and we talked. He offered me anything I needed.

Then I sat wondering what to do next. I looked over and saw a kid my brother had gone to school with, then I wrote a note to a rabbi, explaining that I'm by no way perfect, but I am trying to understand life. There has to be more to life than this; otherwise, why bother having life at all? I also asked for help finding a place to go learn about Judaism, in order to learn more about myself.

I gave notice at work, telling the restaurant manager I was going to get my Master's degree. He was cool about everything. I worked up until the day I left, and we were cool as far as I knew. Just like that, I was on my way to Israel to study in a yeshiva (kind of like a university, but only with dudes).

First, I got some basic learning from a local rabbi, and then started contemplating life in general, to figure out if any part was worth keeping. I couldn't really find anything.

Chapter 13
Bye Bye Memphis, Hello Jerusalem

Not knowing what laid ahead for me, I began my journey with all kinds of chaos. Before I left, a friend had given me a special joint, to smoke before I boarded the plane. As I boarded the plane, it hit me like a bullet! I was tripping something fierce, there was no way I was sleeping through this flight.

The only directions I had to the place I was going to in Israel were: go to the Wailing Wall in Jerusalem, then ask for directions. Not a problem. When I arrived in Chicago and switched planes, I found out that drinks were free on international flights. Now me still partying like a rock star, because that was just how I rolled, and that Canadian band "Tickle Back" hadn't coined the term yet, I pimped as much whiskey as I could get on that flight. I drank so much that the stewardess asked me to follow her, and as instructed, I went to the back of the plane.

I thought, "Crap, I'm going to get arrested." Instead, she told me to sit down, because if I was going to drink all flight, she didn't want to keep walking back and forth. I drank to my heart's content and made my way to London, where I had a four hour layover. I visited this Scotch store; I forgot the name, but they offered free samples.

So I boarded my next flight, which wasn't so bad: on this one, I kept a steady diet of vodka and tonics, with the occasional pretzel. Now, when most people arrive in the Holy Land for the first time, they kiss the ground or say a prayer. I was debating what to do as they parked on the tarmac and began deboarding.

Me, growing up questioning authority was natural, and my experiences in life taught me three things:
3) Always be aware of your surroundings
2) Always look someone in the eye when talking to them
1) When being stared at, always stare back until they break eye contact
Following these rules, I began to exit the plane.

Walking down the steps, I noticed four police officers, three soldiers, and about five security officers walking with a slight haste, and it looked like they were heading towards me. At the time, my hair was just below my shoulders, and my beard was just as long. I got approached by the man before I got off the steps of the plane, telling me to come with them. I did as they asked, then the questions started coming out of left field.

"Where are you from?"

"Memphis."

"Your passport says California and New Orleans."

"Memphis doesn't have a passport office, so I had to go through the one in New Orleans."

"Why did you move from California to Memphis? Where is this Memphis? Near Miami?"

"No."

"Is it near New York, LA, Chicago?"

"No, it's in between New York and Miami," as I did my best to create a map in the air with my hands.

"Why did you come here?"

"To go to yeshiva."

"Do you speak Hebrew?"

"No."

"Can you read Hebrew?"

"No."

"How can you go to yeshiva?"

"They have a beginners program."

"Who is your father?"

"My father died four years ago. Thanks for bringing that up."

"What did he do?"

"I don't know, I'm tired, I haven't slept, and I haven't had a cigarette in a while. Do you mind if I smoke?"

"Yes, I mind. You can go."

I started my stride towards the buses that take you to the terminal. I got about four steps, when I heard, "Where are you from?"

"Memphis, Tennessee, home of the King."

"The King?"

"Yes, Elvis Presley."

"Who is this?", at which point I got pissed: you can not know a lot of things in this world, but not knowing who Elvis Aaron Presley was is just an insult.

Then the questions really started to fly out.

"Who is your father, and what does he do?"

"He is dead, and I never met him. My mother told me he was a mailman."

"Why did you come to Israel?"

"To learn about being Jewish."

"Are you Jewish?"

"Yes, do you want to see my bris?"

"Why do you need to learn about being Jewish if you are already Jewish?"

"So I can better understand myself."

"You wait here." The radio went beep, and some language that sounded like Hebrew came over the air. Then the man said, "Where will you be staying?"

"In Jerusalem, near the wall."

"Which wall?"

"I don't know, my brother told me just to go to the wall and ask for the place."

"You should plan better when traveling. It isn't smart not to think ahead."

"I live my life day by day, hour by hour, and when the shit hits the fan, I don't freak out, dude."

"Okay, you can go. Maybe you should shave your beard."

That pissed me off, so I responded with a customary insult from America: I told him to mind his own damn business and gave him the finger. Then I mumbled something about his mother doing a donkey show in Tijuana and hopped on the bus that goes to the terminal.

It's just me at this point, with about nine soldiers and two police officers. I get off, and two plainclothes gentlemen were trotting towards me and started in with the "who's your daddy" crap. I told them my dad died four years ago, and I really can't tell them anything else about him, because I don't know what you want to know about him. He drank

70

single malt Scotch and loved a good bottle of vodka. The guy then replied something in Hebrew that I understood to mean I was crazy, so I lit up a cigarette and offered him one.

Five minutes later he asked me what I did back home, so I told him I was a professional football player and had a bum knee. He asked why I smoked, and I told him if he had a mother like mine he'd understand. He laughed and said, "I think I smoke for the same reason: Jewish mothers. Come inside now."

I entered the building to see all kinds of lines snaking all over the place. Just when I got into the right line, I got pulled out by security and asked for my passport and told to follow him. So there I went, into some side office with four Russian women, yelling at the top of their lungs at me, and I couldn't make out anything they said. One of them asked me for the phone number of the place I was going, so I gave it to her. She dialed, no one picked up, and so more yelling. The big question they were arguing over was, "Are you Jewish?"

"Yes, do want to see my mark?" As I stood up to unzip my pants, she started laughing. Then she explained to the others what I was doing, and they all laughed as well. She told me a secret that I should know about Israelis: "We are like candy: hard on the outside, but soft and sweet on the inside. You just have to know this, and you will understand us."

So she told me that once they talk to somebody at the school, they will let me go. In the meantime, she started to drill me about Americans. I told her I'm not typical, but let me know if you want to get some coffee some time. Well, then she sent one of the girls out for coffee and asked if I needed a smoke. The answer was, "Of course."

"Let's go," she said. We had a quick coffee break and chit-chatted a bit. Then she said, "Okay, you can go. If you need help, call me, I will talk to them for you." So back to the line to get my passport stamped I went.

Five minutes later two guards came up to me, and I pointed to her office and yelled her name. She came out, yelling and screaming, and put those guys in their place. I eventually got my passport stamped and got my bags, only to get stopped again. This time, they asked to search my bags. They were full of clothes and an alarm clock that had just started buzzing. Yeah, that took another hour, as they insisted a supervisor come with the portable X-ray unit to check it for bombs and more questions.

"Where is this Memphis place?"

I hold out my hands and say, "New York, Chicago, Miami, LA, Memphis."

"Is it a big city?"

"It's not that big, but not exactly small."

"Well, which is it big or small? I don't think you are from a city, if you can't tell if it is big or small."

"It's in the middle, moron. What do you mean big? Population? Square Feet? How tall the buildings are? Which is it, huh?"

"You don't like it when I ask you questions, do you? Well, do you?"

At this point, he looked like his head was going to blow a gasket, and another man came up and asked me why my hair was long. I gave him the standard answer: "Because I work so much, the barber is never open when I'm awake." Confused, he asked why I didn't do it myself. I told him that I didn't think my hair warranted a letter of condemnation from the UN Security Council.

I finally got out of the airport, and it's around 7 pm. My flight had landed at 6:45 in the morning, so I was kind of pissed off, but what the hell, I got a girl's number. And she was in uniform, which was just plain hot.

I finally arrived in the Old City of Jerusalem with a bunch of bags around 9 pm and not really sure where to go. I began asking everybody walking by where this place was, and everybody acted like they didn't speak English. I was just about to pimp slap the next person that said, "I don't know, I don't speak English," in a New York accent.

So I began lugging all my stuff towards the nearest shop, and I finally found somebody who asked me where I was going. I explained my situation, and he laughed, saying, "I teach there, let me give you a hand."

This was my first day in Israel, and that just pissed me off to the point I wanted to go grab a soldier's gun and open fire on every last person in my general vicinity. Welcome to the Holy Land.

Chapter 14
Working for the Man

I get checked in with the school and was sent to the dorm. Lucky for me, I was placed in the penthouse: I had a view of the Temple Mount from my room, and from the roof, all of the Old City. I began going to basic classes, learning things that I should have known but didn't. They were extremely helpful, and they helped me learn that no matter my past, it's never too late to turn my life around.

Now, you must understand, I normally don't have an accent, but surrounded by New Yorkers and some folks from LA, my Southern pride was not going to be questioned by some damn Yankees. I let my "y'alls" and "reckons" fly, slowed down a bit and relaxed my tongue while talking. I continued to use this everywhere I went, with the exception of the South.

Miles, an ex-Australian rules football player, kept asking me about Texas. I sat him down and laid it out: never ask a Tennessean if they are from Texas, that's just an insult. The sitting governor of Tennessee, named Samuel Houston, got drunk one day after his wife passed away, married some Indian squaw, and ran off to Texas to start a new country. Texas wouldn't be there had it not been for those brave Tennesseans that died in the Alamo. In fact, I wager had there been one more Tennessean present at that battle, they would have fended off the rest of Santa Anna's epic army.

The lecture I gave convinced people I was a backwoods hick. No problem, I played it up, because I'd rather be a hick than a carpet-bagging Yankee without common courtesy. Soon enough people started calling me Tennessee. I didn't object, and in fact I took pride in my new name. I met some cool people my first few weeks there, and I began a Friday ritual of remembering everything I learned that week and trying to apply it to my life.

I also spent the afternoons listening to 80s pop and old school country with headphones on, dancing on the roof top and watching the hajji's throw rocks down onto my people praying at the wall. This was followed by police in riot gear going up to the Temple Mount and shooting tear gas into that Golden Dome, and teenagers using old ladies as shields to throw rocks and run. This happened every Friday.

I considered myself to be a peaceful guy, following Rodney King's epic quote, "Can't we all just get along?" This, as I soon learned, wasn't an option, as I took my first bus ride on the public bus. I was on the bus for about 10 minutes before a soldier got on and said something to me. Once again not breaking eye contact, I told him I speak English. He said passport. I gave it to him, and he walked off the bus and motioned with his M-16 to follow him. I got off the bus, and it leaves, then comes the questions: who is your father, what does he do, you know the drill.

After about 20 minutes, he says I can go, and guess what? I don't have enough money to get back on the damn bus. I had to hoof it about two hours, but I made it, and I learned a lesson: buses were going to be a pain in the ass, but not nearly as bad as walking everywhere.

I spent my free time in the Old City town square people watching. Well, after a while, people became infatuated with the notion of a Jewish kid from Memphis, Tennessee. I soon began telling people I was from the home of the Moshiach of Rock 'n Roll (Moshiach meaning king, often misunderstood for Jesus). Either way, I was making friends, melting the ice with Israelis, but still getting yanked off buses and searched at nearly every turn.

Then the holiday known as Purim came along, which is kind of like Halloween for Jews, as far as getting drunk and wearing costumes goes. I figured its time I went for the gold: I went to an over-grown public garden in the Old City and found some thorns. I made a crown out of weaving several branches together, and when I put it on, it even stuck me. Then I broke two big sticks and made a cross, attached it to my back with a belt, tossed my old poncho on and put some nails in between my fingers.

I made it into the yeshiva wearing this outfit, and half of the people were rather upset, the other half loved it. Then I performed a skit, thanks to South Park for the "Okay, everybody turn around. Behold, it's a miracle!" move, as candy came flying down from the heavens. When I got done there, I began walking back to my dorm, when a soldier spotted me, started laughing, and begged me to let him lead me around the city at gun point. Very politically incorrect, but funny as Hell, so I let him lead me, and soon the rest of his unit spotted me and joined the party. This was the last time I was harassed on a bus or just for walking minding my own business.

A lot of people had a hard time with my accent, because I took my time when I spoke, like each word I said had a purpose and a meaning, not just cannon fodder like those fools from up North. Me and the British guys got along, as they didn't like New Yorkers any more than I did, and most of the people over nineteen thought I was the genuine article.

I devoted myself to learning, even while walking around and admiring the beauty of the land. Despite my apparent lack of civilized education, I was still capable of having a conversation in my head, debating what I had learned while walking and smoking a cigarette, which made asking questions later more fun, despite the craving for nicotine. Not to be all self-centered, but I was doing this because I wanted to be a better man.

I know that concept escapes a lot of people, but I took it to heart. The idea that perhaps I could be a better man tomorrow than I was the day before, and I did my damnedest to make sure not to repeat the same mistakes day in and day out. I listened to the song "Hurt" sung by Johnny Cash on repeat in my head, and it gave me a new take on life. I remember my grandmother reminding me that money isn't the most important thing in the world, and if it ever became the only reason you're doing something, it will make you miserable.

I remembered the fight that got me kicked out of Boy Scouts: it was an argument over who should be respected more, the guy flipping burgers at McDonald's, or the rich guy who sits on his butt all day. Keep in mind, growing up without a father, I was automatically considered "the evil one", and, since I was poor, people had no problem with blackballing me.

Money was never my driving force in life, but I still needed some. So I began babysitting and cleaning apartments, working anywhere I could so I could stay in Israel longer. If that makes me all about the money, I would ask you, did Bill Gates ever scrub toilets for a pack of cigarettes and some laundry money? I knew I could always call Big Mo, and the next day Western Union would have cash for me, but I also knew that lifestyle would kill me, one way or another, so I severed ties with a bunch of people in order to live a clean life, one that I could be happy with.

Now, I met some guys who were devoted to helping me accomplish this goal, and others who reminded me of what I was missing out on. After a while, I shaved my beard: it was itching way too much for me to handle, but I kept the long hair. Remarkably, no more harassment from people, and somehow the girl who worked at the bagel shop was giving me the "I like you but I don't speak English" discount when it came to coffee and bagels.

Now, scrubbing toilets might not sound like fun, but I actually felt better about myself at the time. I would go out for pizza and beer from time to time. Every now and then a Cuban cigar, and a cheap bottle of vodka, then just howl at the moon while listening to some power ballads and trying to fix all the problems in the world. Life was good.

From time to time, a new kid would come in and ask my story, which put me in an awkward place, because I would tell my story and then the people would want to get blitzed with me. I would try to remind people that I wasn't doing that stuff anymore, but who was I kidding, I was one good Scotch away from hitting on everything that walked. I had been invited to a wedding over my time there, and, well, the Scotch was good. A nice single-malt combined with cheap wine makes for one hell of a party.

On the walk back with a few English soccer hooligans, we were rather loud and didn't care much for civility, or people. It was close to 2 in the morning, and we're all sitting around the square, when I spot two ladies sitting on the other side of the square. I did what came naturally to me and waved them over. Being Israeli, they did get that I meant for them to come over, but they mocked my wave, so I went over and joined them. They were cool, one of them totally got my hippie persona, and she also went nuts for my accent.

We exchanged numbers, and just my luck, she was stationed in the Old City. This made life interesting for me, being in a yeshiva, and walking around the Old City with some guys, and then a unit of girl soldiers would walk by all, "Hi Jeff! Hey Jeff! We love Jeff", and my personal favorite "Jeff, come take tour with us!" I would get a text with a mix of Hebrew and English words in a combination of lettering, which took me the better part of an hour to try to translate before responding. Then we would meet up and talk; she would teach me some Hebrew, and I would teach her some Southern folklore.

It was nothing fancy. She was cute, but I was more interested in her than her looks, which was a step in the right direction for me. She would help with my reading and writing, and then we would just sit and look at the sky, on top of some random building. Pretty soon, the girl from the bagel shop asked me out, and it was kind of the same deal. I felt like crap kind of dating two girls, but not really dating anyone.

This made yeshiva life difficult, because people thought I was chasing tail. If I was chasing tail, I would have never been seen near the yeshiva or talking to anyone wearing black. It just happened that I wasn't one of those guys who pretended that women don't exist, when they are going out of their way not to look or talk to them. I would talk to anybody, and if they had a cigarette or bottle, I'd be theirs all night! Still, I showed up the next day and gave my undivided attention to the rabbis, trying to internalize the lessons of the day.

I never claimed to be perfect, it just so happened I was going out with both girls, and they both knew what was going on, but weren't fussy about it, it was just whatever it was. What. Ever. I love those two words. With those two words, I picked a fight with a guy, and instead of me getting a punch or a kick thrown at me, a soldier walked up and ordered him to take a hike, and then bought me a shot.

I had never met this soldier before, but he knew me: he had seen me on the tours around town that were meant for soldiers only. He laughed, and we talked over a beer. He informed me that he had to transfer my soldier girl, because it was time and she didn't want to tell me, so he volunteered to break the news. However, I was invited to the base for her going-away party the next night. Me and the bagel girl were still tight, and we were smoking the hookah in the middle of the afternoon when the soldier girl came running up to me, crying on my shoulder. It turned out Yasser Arafat had died, and war was going to start, or at least she thought, and she was very worried.

Now me, I can't stand the notion that a terrorist could win the Nobel Peace Prize. She was so worried, she was shaking. The three of us went on a walk, talking and joking, trying to lighten the mood. In the back of my mind still rested the fact that the enemy is the reason the Sbarro is closed at the moment, and, yeah, I was standing about 100 yards from the place where one of my "peaceful" cousins blew himself up, killing innocent pizza-loving folks.

We spent the next three days talking. The bagel girl went to work, and me and the soldier girl went to her family's home to break the news to her parents. I didn't sign up for this drama, it just happened I cared for that girl and still do. My fondest memory of us was on the bus ride back: we were the only ones aboard, and I taught her how to sing "I'm a Yankee Doodle Dandy". Why? I don't know, don't question me.

I went to her going-away party on base, and I was stuck inside of a small office with 20-odd female soldiers, all with M-16's pointed at me. It was kind of a rush, but better than the alternative. She spoke her parting words to the group and told them they had to take care of me. And not to let the Arab police force get on me for smoking hash, because if I had some, I would share it with them. This came out of nowhere! I never once mentioned drugs or drug usage, but I guess my reputation preceded me.

Just like that, what was meant to be wasn't, and I was walking down the road alone again. A few days later, I'm walking with one of the head rabbis of the yeshiva, and the whole gaggle of female soldiers came walking by, doing the "We love you Jeff! High Five!" thing. Of course, the high fives were just innocent, but the rabbi took offense. He was try to explain this practice called "Shomer Negia", which means "guarding your touch". In other words, he was afraid me touching their hands would lead me to do deviant things.

I was just giving them a high five! Meanwhile, me and the bagel girl were doing good. I proposed to her one night, then she asked me where would we live? I told her I would make a tent, because I'm a Survivalist™, and that's just how I roll. She said, yes, I suppose the notion of living in a tent is irresistible, and she didn't mind that her parents hated me (her mom thought I was trying to steal her and take her back to America).

One thing led to another, and she wound up getting word from somebody that I would be better off without her. Looking back now, I can't answer that. I saw her the last time I was in Jerusalem. She had stroller built for three and was happily married. That eased my guilt.

As for the soldier girl, well, most people just assumed we stopped talking. Not really the case. You see, she went down to a touristy town in the Sinai Peninsula for Passover one year. Well, it just so happened that so did one of those filthy Arab scum bags with bomb and nails attached to his chest went down there, too. She's alive, but the most peaceful person I had ever met was left with half of her face and only a quarter of her eye sight. She isn't the same person, and won't be. The last time we talked, she told me about her living nightmare, which reminded me of a scene from "Apocalypse Now". She now lives in a constant terror that forced her into a mental hospital.

For this alone, I want to kill all of the pig-faced, goat-humping, elephant-breathed Muslims in the world, but that wasn't her way. She didn't understand war, nor did she want to. In the words of John Lennon, her philosophy sounded something like the lyrics to "Give Peace a Chance". That's what she would have wanted, and for that I hold my rage inside whenever I see one of those camel-jockey, wife-beating, shit for brains Muslims walking around.

It's still a painful subject for me every now and then. In my time there, I met several people and learned more and more about my history, which enabled me to learn about myself, and soon I began to really understand the lessons that were handed down from generation to generation. I did feel better about myself after a while, but with that confidence, I got to be cocky. Humility is one of things I have, but when it comes to people, I prefer them to adapt to me, as opposed to me adapting to them. It was destined for me to fall from grace; it was just bound to happen. The trick was for me not to fall too far down.

One of the people I studied with on a regular basis was a former producer, and his wife a dancer and actress. She was going to put on a show in America and do a tour. Since we were learning well together and his kids liked me, I offered to be the roady and drive from town to town and help set up. This made sense to him, too, and we decided to get a RV. This way, the family and nanny could sleep, while I drove all night. There was still time before this was going to happen, but some people at the yeshiva got upset, and while I wasn't in the mood to run drugs or even buy any, it just kind of followed me around.

I never got in trouble for it, but I did feel bad for a little bit. Every time I went to a wedding, I felt out of place. So extremely out of place to the point that it was uncomfortable for me, so I would drink to excess and leave late or when the bar was empty.

While all this was going on, I found a book: it's kind of a guideline to the strictest views in Judaism. With this book, I took a test that was given to potential rabbis as a final exam, and I aced the damn test. I had to rip it up, because being a rabbi means you are willing to take on a leadership role in one way or another, and that was not for me. I just wanted to get to know my people, and hopefully myself. I actually forbade the person who graded the test from telling anybody. I don't regret that decision, but I do regret not rubbing it in the faces of a couple of people who didn't think I did anything but talk to anybody walking around.

I was fortunate to have study partners who knew better and realized I was capable of thinking about more than one thing at a time. I felt like once I announced I was leaving for a while, people got upset and had no desire to see me anymore. Before I left, I met with the head of the yeshiva in his office. Most people consider this a great honor; I was not one to disagree.

When I met with him, he was cool. He asked me what I was going to do, and when I told him, he told me to go with God. He asked me what had I learned? I told him I would need more time, but, most importantly, I did learn there is a God, and He had a plan for us all, and I'm not one to question His methods anymore. He laughed and said that he still questions His methods, and then he asked me to pray twice a day. Not even pray: his exact words were, "Talk to God two times a day, and you will be better for it."

I do appreciate the reassurance I got from him, which I had gotten from some of the rest of the people. But coming from the head rabbi, it meant a lot more than a certificate saying I was a rabbi.

Chapter 15
The Tour

My friend Todd had produced a one woman show for his wife, and we were going to share her message with the rest of the world, or at least most of the American Jewish community. Her show was about her journey in life from being a Rockette to a nice Jewish housewife, who happened to be Japanese. We were going to do shows in NY, LA, and everywhere in between, and out of the way, too. Now, he and his wife were very religious; I wasn't quite there, but it didn't matter. Out of respect for him and his family, I did the best I could on the religion thing.

Anyway, I met him in Brooklyn after a quick visit home that was uneventful, except for catching up with some friends. Off to the Big Apple, a place I hadn't been to since I was like 12, and for good reason. I didn't like the pace or the people; I was always a fish out of water, and the thought of driving around town scared me, not for fear of life, but for fear of having to talk to one of those Yankees. My promise to my grandmother would be safe.

I hated the hustle and bustle of the Big Apple. The lack of common courtesy among people made my small acts of random courtesy seem like a big deal. I held open an elevator door for an old lady with groceries, and the other people on the elevator started cussing at me. I opened a door for a lady walking in to a Starbucks and that was a no-no, I found out, because she gave me some women's lib-crap.

We started off by driving a cargo van around getting ready for the trip. It took a while. Todd wasn't an easy person to work for, but I knew that he wasn't really a jerk, it was just the job. In fact, he fired a girl before she even started and hired a nanny within a few days, because the first lady didn't like kids. This made life easier, but meant I had to do all the setup, driving, some promotion, and, most importantly, watch the two kids during the show.

Now, I was intimidated by the RV and 7-foot trailer at first, and in the city, it was nightmare. Soon, I came to grips with the situation: I was bigger than the other cars, and I didn't care if they weren't going to let me over, because they would. Before a show, I found a parking spot right in front of the building, took up five metered spaces, and when a meter maid came walking by, I just put quarters in all the meters just in front of her. It was funnier at the time, because my orange hair was flowing through a bandana, and she yelled at me for taking up all the spots.

Then she asked me where she knew me from. She said, "You're an actor, aren't you? I saw you in a movie. Which one was it?"

I decided it would be cooler to tell her I was in a bad movie. This way it wouldn't matter much: she wouldn't want to go get the movie and find out I was full of shit. It hit me: I told her I was in the "Whole 9 Yards" with that guy from "Friends". She asked for an autograph, I gladly gave her my mark, and went for a walk.

The next thing I know, we were just outside of Boston, on the way north. We were staying at people's houses on the Sabbath and visiting different communities. After a while, I got tired of telling my story, so I would try not to get too close to the people we were staying with.

We were on our way towards Canada for a show in Montreal, and then to Toronto. Now, I would get a few days off from time to time, and when I did, I played my favorite drinking game. I called it Subway Roulette: I would get an all-day pass, hop on a random train, get off, find the nearest bar, pound a beer, and hop back on the subway. After seven or eight stops, hop off, and enjoy the place I was at.

I had a blast whenever I walked into a new bar. People would stare at me kind of funny, and in Canada, I reminded them they picked the wrong person to mess with. Some old guy made a comment about my shirt which read "Jesus did it for the Chicks", and I threw an empty bottle of Molson's Import at his head. He started to charge, and I stuck my foot out as I sidestepped, and he went face first into the ground. I politely stuck my foot on the back of his neck and asked him if wanted to go outside, or buy me a beer? He bought me a beer, and the Southern accent got me invited back to someone's house.

This was just flat out weird: I had my beer-goggles on, and the place was dimly lit. Anyway, back at her house, I was about to join her in the bedroom, when I realized she wasn't a tasty senorita, she was a senior citizen! I went to the bathroom, looked in the mirror, and made a dash for the door. Now, having to put my snow pants and boots on made it interesting, as I could hear her calling my name, as I fell down the stairs while pulling my snow pants up. I landed rough, but it was better than the alternative.

Montreal in February had snow piled about 15-feet on the side of the roads, and the salt on the ground would tear up carpet and the bottom of your shoes. I started back to the place I was staying, only I forgot how to get back, so I rode the train and played my game a little longer. Then I walked into a strip club just because I could, and had nothing better to do, since I wasn't sure where else to go.

Sitting in the back of the bar, I noticed one of the girls who knew me when I was playing gangster. She ran up to me and started running her mouth about how she had to run away from her pimp, but now she was in charge, and the owner of the club came up. She introduced me, and he yelled at her, then she whispered something in his ear. I still don't know what she told him. He said, "Walk with me," and we walked. He was telling me all about his club, and how on Friday nights it's a nightmare, because the girls are all on something, fighting and stuff.

I reminded him that he chose this business, the business didn't choose him, and to look at the bright side: he had a fully stocked bar and naked women walking around. What more did he want out of life? With that we sat down and polished off bottle after bottle, and then he got the nerve to ask me if I was still juggling four or five girls a night.

I told him that it seemed a lot cooler at the time, but it was a nightmare having to deal with all their crap. Then he asked if I wanted a job: he needed a DJ, and someone to help him manage the place. I thought long and hard for the next 10 seconds, and told him I couldn't do it. That life was over for me. I then proceeded to get hammered with him, and the girl I knew came up to me, sat on my lap, and I told her about the old lady. She was loving that story, and then she rolled a phatty blunt. We went out back to smoke, because she didn't want any of those "whores" getting in on her stuff.

When we got back inside, the owner was in the DJ booth and said the girl was up next. I told her, "I got this," and went into the booth. I picked out the perfect stripper songs for her: "Closer" by Nine Inch Nails, followed by "Free Bird". Why Free Bird? Dude, be serious, it's freaking "Free Bird", it's always the perfect song. Then I left, not quite remembering where I was staying. The next morning, Todd asked me where I was and what I had done. I told him it was just one of those Jack and Coke nights, and we laughed. That was it.

Next stop Toronto, so I played my game again, this time with a twist: I would do a shot instead of a beer. Well, the next morning, I woke up outside the RV in the snow, and that's all I remember. Some will say I was living a double-life, or being a hypocrite, I never looked at it like that. I have vices, and I make mistakes, but I'm not the only one. I was working really hard, I was going on a couple hours sleep a day, setting up the stage, wiring, lights, speakers, and then watching the kids during the show, or selling CDs after, then packing up, and driving to the next city. So when I got a night off, I took advantage. Maybe I had too much fun, but when I work hard, I play hard, that's just how I live my life. It just kind of happens; I never planned to do anything.

In Toronto, I bought some Cuban cigars and some whiskey. Next stop was Detroit, so crossing the border made for some great times, as I pulled up in the RV, and the border patrol was just convinced I was dirty. I wrote on the form I bought cigars and whiskey, so they made everybody get up and out of the RV and searched it. Unfortunately, my boss had a safe and a lot of cash from all the shows, and that just led to us being treated like drug smugglers.

They went through everything and started complaining about my cigars, and Fidel, and I was going to have to either smoke them now, or flush them down the toilet. After they X-rayed everything, they let us go with an official warning. So now I get harassed for smuggling whenever I pass at an airport. Just a quick heads up: always keep the Cubans in your pocket, and you'll be fine. They never search your pockets in customs.

Back to driving around. I went through Chicago, and I was pretty tame, until I picked up a cowboy hat somewhere in Georgia, when we did some shows in Atlanta. I passed through Memphis and got my CDs. This made it a party, and driving at night was a blast. Savannah was by far the coolest place that I wish I could have hung out more at and done some damage there. That place just had a special feel to it, and it was beautiful: my accent wasn't so bad there. But it wasn't in the cards, as we had to be in Miami the next day.

I drove straight through the night, only stopping twice for gas and a quick cigarette. I had cruise control on, my feet out the window, some Eric Clapton in the CD player, and 80 miles an hour was just fun. Once we got in, I crashed, and then I recall seeing my aunt at the West Palm show. Miami was strange: because of the time of the show and booking arrangements, I had to stay close, so that right after the Sabbath, I could do all the set up.

I stayed at some hotel and did some grocery shopping for myself: a bottle of Scotch and some herring. I went to services Friday night, hoping to find a meal. For the first time I was at Chabbad Temple, and nobody even said hello to me. Chabbad is one of those interesting sects of Judaism I never quite understood. I opted to go back, and being alone in a hotel, I just fired up some smokes, drank some Scotch, and turned on the TV. This was first time in about a year and a half that I had broken the Sabbath.

After Miami, we went through the "Redneck Rivera" for a show, and then onto New Orleans, where I was a good boy. From there, off we went to Houston or Dallas, I can't remember. Then onto Denver, which was very important, because I had left some stuff in the basement after we lost the car on the road trip. I collected my stuff, mainly the rest of my CD collection, my pride and joy, with over 2,000 CDs. From Denver, we took the scenic route through Utah, on the way to Vegas.

Now I will say, Utah has some of the most beautiful scenery in world. But I had no time to stop, had to make it to LA for a show. We got to LA, and I found out that we only had to set up once and take down once, since the shows were going to be in the same place. I took a quick trip to San Fran to visit my aunt and my cousin, made a side trip to Berkley to pick up another copy of Mao's book and some other communist materials, before making my way back to LA.

Once back in LA, I went to visit my favorite hair dresser, Raymond. He did my hair on the side of the road, and we went to a club. I had people coming up, convinced I was a movie star. The reason had more to do with my attitude, and the fact that the last time I was in LA, I bumped into Matthew Perry at the Grove. More like he bumped into me, and I spilled my drink.

He apologized by taking me inside and buying me a beer at the bar. He then proceeded to laugh during our quick conversation. He said, "I don't envy you tonight, man. Live it up!" He then said, "I'll see you on set next week. Don't forget, we start shooting at 2 pm." He then walked off, and every bartender, waitress, seamstress, model, and actress in the bar was in my lap. The drinks came free; the bartender wanted me to pass his head shot along.

The actress/model who worked for Liz Claiborne won my heart that night. I wound up going to her place and just hanging out with her. She was introducing me to models, hairdressers, fashion designers, as I was starring in a new movie with Mr. Perry, the guy from "Friends". I got free clothes, designer stuff, and all the velvet ropes were opened for me.

I went into a club with her, and they sat us in a booth next to Leonardo and Tobey. Well, this place was charging $800 for a bottle of Grey Goose. I didn't have the cash, but they did, and the model chick threw me into their booth, and we partied with them. When she left, I couldn't help but tell them what was going on. They loved it; in fact, they played it up even further for me by telling her that I might be in their next projects.

Then she refused to let me go or leave her side, and everywhere we went, it was free. I actually got tired of the popularity, the rat race, real quick. Then I made the worst decision in the world: I told her the truth, and in the blink of an eye, I was on the curb. But I had a white Armani, and the velvet ropes were still open when I left.

So upon returning to the Grove a little older and wiser, some people remembered me, and just like that, I was giving people my mark on random stuff and posing for pictures with people. Now the model chick refused to talk to me and couldn't have people knowing she got played. So my rep was intact; I just blamed the studio for sitting on the films I was in.

Then I just let the bullshit fly from there because I could, on the spot. When I was younger and staying with my uncle in Malibu, I spotted Michael Keaton at a taco place and said, "That's Batman!" He corrected me, and then told me to notice that he was trying to play down who he was, so as not to be hassled. In fact, he was driving a beat-up Chevy. The lesson was, sometimes when you're a star, you try not to get noticed. I did the playing down thing so well that while sitting on some steps smoking a cigarette outside of a club, some guy parked his car and gives me a 10-spot, because he thought I was homeless. I took his money back into the club as I walked by him in line, and said, "Good luck getting in, dude."

Then I gave the "What Up, G" double-pat chest-bump double-pump bro-hug to the bouncer and told him not to let that guy in. Jackass, insulting me. Back in the club, I bumped into a few stars, and since I acted like I owned the night, they hung out with me, bought me drinks. I hooked up with another model that night, but it wasn't long before I had to hit the road again.

I had only a few days to get from LA back to New York in a rental truck. I hit the open road solo, feet out the window, cigarette in my hand, and 90 mph through Utah, to Colorado, with a blizzard chasing me down. Oh yeah, by the way, only in Utah will you see a beautiful blonde 16 year-old girl pumping gas.

I was flying up the mountain, with snow all over the road, just like it was nothing, changing lanes and what not. Then I flew down the mountain, swerving past cops, who had pulled over. I didn't care. Flying from town to town, I stopped in Omaha for the night, stayed with the rabbi, who was pretty cool.

Then I made it to New York earlier than planned, and it was all good. We had some more shows to do there, but I had a lot of free time, and, well, I made my presence known in Manhattan with authority. I walked into the Waldorf Astoria, acted like I owned the place. Went to the bar, drank up a storm, got the bill, just signed it, and put a random room down. That wasn't my first drink and dash, nor would it be my last.

I managed to get into some dive bars that only the hipsters knew about. I had a nice rep going there in the city that never sleeps. I managed to convince people I was a roady for Slash, but the bastard had just fired me. This actually got me a bar backing job for the night, made close $700 in tips. After a while, we finished the show. I packed up and made my way back to Memphis, on the way to Seattle again, to work for my brother.

Chapter 16
Seattle

So my older brother got his first catering job at, like 12 years old; you could say he always knew what he wanted to do. He started his kosher catering and restaurant business when he was 20, just after he got married. Now he put me to work, because my mother told him I needed the job; I went to work for him because my mother told me he needed the help: we both got conned by our mother, who is legally insane.

Working for him was interesting, because I had been a restaurant manager, and I had also held almost every job possible in the restaurant business. A typical day would start around 4:30 am or so, and the restaurant closed around 9 pm, which meant it was possible to finish by 11, but probably wouldn't be out the door 'til 1 on a good day. Now, if there happened to be a catering event, there was no way of telling when I would get off.

I was staying at my sister-in-law's parents' house. On the Sabbath, I would spend it with them or my brother, or both. None of these things were a problem, it's just when you're doing that type of work, it gets old quick. The only friend I had was Jorge, the chef. We understood each other, and we hated the hours and the drama. When we would have somewhat of a free night, we would go out for drinks and from time to time shoot some pool.

The life was just too damn repetitive for me. It wasn't the money, or even scrubbing floors. It was the pace, lack of sleep, and, above all else, the feeling of being alone in the world that I hated. It wasn't like I could just start dating or move out: I hardly had free time to get a haircut. Some of the Mexicants I worked with were cool, but the cycle sucked: making deliveries to fancy hotels, ballparks, convention centers, ballrooms, Microsoft corporate offices, and stuff just got to be a pain in the ass, and it wasn't fun or rewarding in any way for me.

I didn't like the snobs I ran into, and I spent what little free time I had at the casinos. I won a little money, but for me it was just a place to escape for an hour or two to wind down, so I could get some sleep. I wasn't sure how to deal with any of this stuff; I just knew I was miserable. I figured out what Kurt Cobain was thinking when he shot himself. Something about Seattle just makes people feel icky and depressed.

I would go to a few college bars and some Microsoft bars, but none of them were any fun. I couldn't buy a good time in that town. I don't know how anybody lives there. I flew to Memphis for my cousin's wedding, and my brother didn't want to deal with the kids or our lunatic mother. I just wanted to get away. I figured it might change my attitude.

I got to Memphis on a Thursday, and I had to find a tux for the black tie wedding at the Peabody Hotel. If you don't know Memphis, the Peabody is our old school grand hotel, where rich people like to show off for each other and, of course, they have ducks that play follow the leader once or twice a day through the lobby and into the fountain.

Finding a tux wasn't easy or cheap. I was driving around, passed by a tux shop, and they had a nice, baby blue tux, and I knew it had to be done. I got the lowdown on the meaning of black tie from the lady at the tux shop, and I got the ruffled shirt, pink bow tie and cummerbund, and white shoes. I got all pimped out, and I tell you I was nervous at first, but if you're gonna do something, you gotta go all out.

I overheard some of the wedding party who didn't know me questioning who would wear that tux to a wedding. It was obvious they had never met me, for if they had they would have known that's just how I roll. Moreover, the photographer loved my tux, because he wore one similar to his prom in the 70s. The florist informed me that I had more balls than anyone he ever met, to get off that elevator and walk past the snickering robots like I owned the damn hotel. I was feeling good, except I hate weddings, and that stuff just feels weird.

I made do, though, as the open bar was nice. I proceeded to get plastered, as people in the lobby were making me pose for pictures with them. At some point I hit the wall and was about to pass out, when someone invited me up to a suite for an after party. That kind of got me rejuvenated.

One of my uncles had to help me out of the hotel, as I was a little too hammered to find the door. I apologized to my aunt and uncle the next day for getting wasted, but that psycho mother of mine had told everybody that I was drugged. The next day, I tried to talk to my aunt and uncle, but they were still pissed and confused about why I would spread rumors about people. That's what happens when one of your parents is psycho.

Should I be upset? Probably not. I went to the same high school as both of my cousins, and neither one of them would give me the time of day. So I guess in their eyes, we weren't related. My other cousin is about to get married now, and I wasn't invited. The psycho mother of my brother is going to make a ruckus, but what do I care?

I flew back to Seattle and showed my brother the wedding pictures. All he could do was laugh. My sister-in-law said she would have cut off my balls had it been her wedding. I continued to work for my brother despite being miserable; I had nothing else to do. Finally, I told him I couldn't do this anymore, and to let me know when a good time to leave would be. I told him I was going to New York, and I was planning on that until I called my uncle in Denver.

I asked him about the offer to send me to Europe, if it still stood. He said yeah, so I took him up on it, and then decided not to tell my brother or anybody else where I was going. I just wanted to be left out on my own. I got some travelers checks and a book about hostels. The day before I left, I helped my brother put some furniture together and helped the father-in-law tar the roof.

It wasn't that I was running away from them. I meant no ill-will, but that lifestyle wasn't for me. I took all my stuff to Goodwill, dropped it off, and then said goodbye to my nieces. I admire my brother for doing what he does, and respect him for being able to, but me, I prefer to be doing something different that makes me happy. I liked the idea of being free and not being a slave to the all-mighty dollar. I reckon that I just needed to get away and see the world.

Now before I left, I stopped by my uncle's in Denver. He was paying for the ticket and offered me money, if I needed it. Well, I spent a lot of my life looking up to him: he had money, women, the life, in my opinion. We talked, and it's just one of those things: you might call it a friend of the moment relationship. I still kept in contact with Lunch Box and Kongo, and that was about it.

I knew one person in London at the time; in fact, he still had my shorts. It took several emails to a mutual friend in Israel to get his phone number. After a pep talk from my uncle that wound up leaving me somewhat depressed, I boarded a plane for London, with a stop in Chicago.

Chapter 17
European Vacation, Tennessee Style

I know, real original taking a backpack to Europe. I got to the airport in Chicago and went out for a cigarette before I boarded the plane. While outside, I started talking with the wheel chair ladies, and I knew I had about 20 minutes until my flight boarded. I looked at the security lane, and I asked the wheel chair lady if she would take me through the lines for $5. She said, "No problem, let me finish my Newport." I went right past the check point line and hobbled through the metal detector, and she pushed me to the gate area.

When I limped up, the stewardess came to me and asked for my boarding pass. I gave it to her, and she ripped it up and gave me a new one in Business Class. She said that it would be more comfortable: it was a long flight, and she was right. Sitting right next to her the whole flight, I got my free drink on. I began hitting on her around my fourth Jack and Coke.

She asked what I did, and I told her I was taking this trip to figure things out. Not the most original, but definitely cool to be doing at my age. She asked what my plans were. I told her I don't make plans, or promises, but I'd love to have dinner with her. She laughed and told me we could do lunch when we landed.

The flight was good, and when we landed, I was the first one off the plane. The customs official was playing the "what are your intentions" game with me. I told him I didn't know how long I was going to be in town, or where I was going to stay. I had a friend who lives out near Wimbley, not real sure where, but he has my shorts, and I plan to get those back. He laughed and asked me how much money I had. I told him around $2,000. He told me I should plan better, and that he was going to give me a 6-month, no-work travel visa. That was cool, then I took off to meet the chick for lunch.

She drove me to a hostel and recommended I stay there, so I checked in, and then we went for some fish and chips. I got her digits and hit the hostel, the Dover Castle or something like that; it was cheap, and they had a bar. I started drinking and talking to the people around there. We had some good conversations, I got the heads up on things, and that night went clubbing with a group of female soldiers and a few tourists.

The next day I hit the museums and did the touristy crap. By stroke of luck, I met an Australian, and we both understood that there are places where a man's worth is determined solely by the amount of alcohol he can ingest in one sitting. We started drinking beer at 3 pm, and at 6 am we were both still up. He finally gave up and surrendered to me. I felt like that was the easiest $20 I'd ever made.

Next day, I met this Italian dame who was awesome, and the only real way for a man like me to score was to make her laugh and act like an asshole. I made this Spanish guy translate my Spanglish into Spanish, and then the Italian guy would translate the Spanish into Italian. Did I mention she spoke English? I kept this going for three days, until I left to reclaim my shorts.

I finally got ahold of a friend of a friend that I had met at this music festival in Israel, called Bombamella. I had one hell of a time getting to the festival: I had to take a bunch of buses and deal with this crazy chick named Gabby. Anyways, at this festival, I came prepared with enough vodka to kill a horse. We would drink, pass out, wake up, hit on this Arab chick in the tent behind us, and I said Arab, not Muslim. We had a great time; her brother offered me three camels and a goat if I married her, but I declined. I would wake up, pop a few pills courtesy of Gabby, smoke a joint courtesy of the Arab, and then mix a tall drink and wander around this festival. It was on that beach where I saw the sexiest thing ever: a 19 year-old chick walking around wearing a bikini and an M-16. I don't think I ever really recovered from that festival, which only had one rule: there are no rules.

I left the festival in Israel a day early, because I had to get back. Somehow in packing, I left a pair of cargo shorts, and now I wanted them back. Not that they were great shorts, but I liked to wear them on hot days. I didn't know what was going to happen. I met my boy at a pub near where he worked, and after a few rounds, he drove me back to his place.

He never told me his father was member of the House of Lords. When I saw the indoor swimming pool, I flipped; then I saw his sister, and the jokes kept coming. I spent my time harassing him about how hot his sister was, and that I would trade him a team of goats for her hand in marriage. The next day while I was in the shower, his maid came and washed all my clothes. As I was getting dressed, the gentleman's gentleman entered and informed me that I was to wear this suit. I put on the suit and figured, okay, I guess I'm going to meet his father today. The gentleman's gentleman gave me a fresh shave, old school barber style, and then he instructed me on how to get to where I was supposed to be.

I was unaware I was supposed to be anywhere, but figured it must be important, so I went along. I told the taxi where I was going. I entered a hotel suite that was packed full of Parliament members and other rich people, when I spotted my friend. He waved me over and told me if I wanted to shake his hand, I should stand in line like this.

I was like, "Who's hand?"

He said, "Prince William's, the future king of England."

I said, "Yeah, I know who he is, dude."

Sure enough, there he was, Prince William with a line of old people waiting to brown-nose him. As the prince was doing his hand shaking, I noticed he was wearing a glove. So I got out of line and went on the balcony for a cigarette. Apparently, my exit caused a ruckus of sorts.

I was soon greeted on the balcony by the prince, who asked why I didn't want to shake his hand. I told him, "Nothing personal, but if I'm going to shake your hand, I prefer to do it with a firm grip, a look in the eye and skin. Gloves take away from what you're really doing when you shake a man's hand."

He asked, "What is that?"

I explained, "You can tell everything you need to know about another man by shaking his hand. You can size him up and measure him, by the grip, the calluses on his hand, and by the look in his eye. Or at least, that is what I take handshakes to be."

He laughed and said, "You have a point," slid the glove off, gave me a firm grip, and made solid eye contact. At this point, it became apparent that I viewed him as my equal, and while I respected his position, it didn't come with my personal respect until he shook my hand.

Afterwards, he asked me where I was going to next on my vacation. I told him I wasn't sure; I was going to meet up with this Australian guy from the hostel, and we would flip a coin. Heads, we go to Edinburgh, tails to Amsterdam. He laughed and said it was a pleasure.

I got back to my friend's house, grabbed my clothes, and got out of that monkey suit, at which point my friend informed me that his father was having to answer for my actions. I apologized and told him I didn't mean to cause any embarrassment. He laughed and said the people who saw him take the glove off and shake a commoner's hand will be telling that story for years to come. He gave me a ride back to the hostel, and I met the Aussie and hit the bus station.

Once there, we flipped a coin: it was Scotland. We got the tickets, and we had a few hours to kill, but he insisted on watching the Ashes (a cricket match between England and Australia). He then proceeded to explain the game of kings to me.

That night, we polished off a bottle of Jack and just kept the party going until we arrived in Edinburgh. We stumbled off the bus like champs and began looking for a hostel. Only problem was, they had this festival in town for performing arts: plays and stuff people from all over the world were in town to see. As we passed one hostel, I noticed a sign that said, "Ask about work for stay."

So I asked the big guy behind the desk, who said, "You clean two hours a day, and you can stay free as long as you do a good job." I said okay, and we began to clean.

After doing this for a few days, I saw a sign for people to work handing out flyers. I went into the office inside of a print shop, beneath a yoga studio, and met Andy. He was cool. He was a bass player, so I told him I was a roadie for Ike Turner and just felt like going solo, hanging out for a while. He put me to work the next day, passing out flyers and hanging posters around the bars and university areas.

I walked into one pub and grabbed a beer. The bartender asked me what was going on, so I told him about being a roadie for Ike Turner, and he insisted that I come hang out with him and his band that night. I made the rounds with him for a while, good people. He introduced me to a Frenchman that needed some work done that wasn't quite legal, but it would pay well. I declined for a while but kept hanging with the Frenchy, because he had tons of women hanging out around him. For being French he was cool, unlike most of the other people from his country.

Now, scrubbing toilets doesn't exactly appeal to most, but I found it relaxing. I didn't mind too much, I just used tons of chemicals. The boss was happy, and I pretty much got my choice of places to clean, who I worked with, and I got to train people. Well one day, I'm sitting around the pool table, and I meet this girl who was drinking Scotch. While we were talking, I discovered she was a nudist, and her boyfriend had been in jail for the past six weeks for refusing to put on clothes when he went before the judge, and he's going to keep going naked until they let him go.

After drinking the night away, she looked at me and asked if I cared to get naughty. I said okay, so we went up to her room, and there were probably eight Japanese tourists sleeping in there. She just turned on the lights, and we went at it. I didn't care, but I felt bad for those people who had to look at my hairy behind.

I went back to my room, passed out around 7 am. I heard her voice in the staff bedroom saying, "Jeff, do you care for a snuggle?" Now, this became a joke for the Aussie who was in the bunk under me. He thought he was dreaming, and after a while, she made me breakfast, and we talked some more. She then told me I was welcome to her car, as she didn't want it any more.

So thus began the torture to follow. For the moment, I was having a blast, and my status as being top drunk was not going to be questioned, especially once I discovered the cheap cider. We are talking really cheap, like "wino in the park fighting with himself shirtless" cheap. I would pound those down while playing pool, and I would talk smack to anybody who was hating America at the time.

A lot of people were hating America, and then one day Katrina came and the pictures on TV were gruesome. Now, hanging out one night in a room filled with Irish folks, I went after the English occupation, and how if they really wanted their freedom, they would fight for it like Americans did, and stop picking potatoes in their free time. I backed myself into a corner with my words, and they were pissed, then I let 'em have it with, "If the Irish didn't waste their time drinking, they might have done something worthwhile, like kick the damn English out of their country, or maybe launch a rocket into outer space, instead of just getting pushed around."

After each insult, I would take a drink, and they slowly realized I was playing my own drinking game. One of the Irish came to understand like the Aussie did, that I was one of the rare breed that understood how to enjoy life with excess partying.

One night, me, this Cornish fellow, and a Canadian were kind of broke and bored. The Canadian had a mandolin, the Cornish dude had a pair of spoons, and I provided the vocals for a group sitting in an alley, singing our hearts out for a few extra pounds. Our hit went a little something like this:

"OOOHHH!!!

I'm stuck here in Edinburgh.

I haven't got a dime,

but if I had a Pound,

I'd by me a bottle of wine."

Now this vocal was heard by the masses walking by, and, well, people were tossing us spare change, cigarettes, and one couple gave us a bottle of wine. We had drunks sitting with us, singing along. It was a night to remember, for at the end of the night we made around 60 pounds each, and a pack of smokes (the wine got drank while we were singing our tune).

This became a ritual, until the owner of the pub next door to us got upset that we were upstaging his juke box. So, passing out flyers got me good exercise, among other things. It also put me in a position to hit on

100

every woman who walked past me, and I could get into the clubs for free.

One night, I bumped into Frenchy, and he asked me to deliver a package to Dover. So I went to pick up the car, dropped off the package, and received another package to take back. I did so, and the car was a piece of crap, but it was free, and I found hitchhikers to pay for gas. Now I got back to Frenchy, he gave me a rather large sum of money, and then I went out for a nice dinner, a few concerts, and made a trip to protest the G-8, where I got tear-gassed and hit with a baton. Worst of all, the car was towed.

It took the rest of the cash to get it out. After that, I made my way back to the hostel. One day, the people from the flyers came by and asked me to help the yoga place with loading their new mats into storage. There I met a nice Jewish-Scot girl, who made me feel bad that I wasn't limber like she was. She gave some free lessons, so to say, and then I bumped into an Israeli on the street, and we started talking. My Hebrew was still pretty bad, but we swapped war stories and info for a few minutes.

I soon developed the urge to drive a bit, so I picked up an Aussie, and we took off. Then we picked up some girls, and, well, I passed out in Barcelona and woke up in Paris. Then we made our way back to Scotland, hanging out with Dirty Dave and Wally. These guys were cool, and they liked the fact I had no regards for social norms.

A few days later, I had been drinking with the Israeli, debating peace and religion, when it occurred to me that maybe I was running away from my spiritual nature by doing all the drugs and crawling into a bottle. Things had to change, but I wasn't sure what to do. At some point, I sold the car for a couple of drinks and some cash.

The next few days were rough, as I had been puking this black stuff every time I ate or drank anything. After three days of this, I went to a hospital at the urging of Dougal, an elderly man, who was just living out his final days at the hostel, so he could be near his daughter. Dougal was full of advice, some for the taking, some for the leaving, but one thing he made clear to me was that you have to live your life, and you can't let others do it for you, or tell you how to do it.

In the hospital, after a few hours, I found out that due to my excessive drinking, my esophagus had swollen shut, and they used a scope to make it wider, but I needed to layoff the booze for a few days. I did as the doctor said and went back to the hostel, and somehow I needed to go home, for I was just tearing up on the inside. I didn't feel right.

I wanted to be a little more productive in making a difference in the world. I still believed that old line from Knight Rider, "That one man can make a difference." So I returned to America, battered and bruised, but ready for a fight.

Chapter 18
Whoops

Upon my return to Memphis with a couple bottles of Scotch and some cookies for my grandmother, my dignity was intact. I went to my grandparents, sat down, talked with them, all was well. They were about to go down to Florida for the winter. I was going to stay at their house for a while and figure some things out. After a week of hanging out with Lunch Box and Kongo, who had moved in together, and Kongo had gotten engaged, Lunch Box was dating, I had little choice but to look for a job or find something to do.

I remembered meeting a guy in Scotland who told me about teaching English in Korea. Now, he had met some of my other friends and was sharing a flat with them. I sent an email asking how to do that, and then I looked into teaching in Korea. All the teaching agency wanted was a college degree and little else. They provided airfare, rent, and paid close to $3,000 a month, which for a single person was enough to live like a king.

I started doing the visa work and dealing with contracts, but not really preparing for what was next. I got hired after less than two weeks, and I was leaving the next week. Now me and my dog were happy hanging out at my grandparents, and I smoked a bowl with her, as her cancer was coming back. I focused all my energy on the spot where her cancer was, attempting to drain it, and take the pain into myself. Why? Because it's a spiritual healing trick I learned from a rabbi, and if I was a jerk, I could have passed it onto another living being, but I'm a man, I could take it.

I went out with Quattro one night before I left, had a great time. I left the dog in my room, so she wouldn't make a mess at my grandparents' house. Well, I got back, and the front door was open: the house had been broken into. I felt like crap.

I called the cops, and then my whacked-out mother to spread the news. The next day, I called my uncle, and then my grandparents. Now they came back from Florida to say goodbye, but my grandfather accused me of breaking into the house, of being the one who stole all their stuff.

This made me furious, even more so than the time I paid my grandmother back money. She had Alzheimer's, and he was in denial about it. A few weeks after he accused me of not paying her back, he took the car that he had given me for graduation and sold it. I wasn't upset; I was pissed! I knew he was an asshole: my grandmother would never let anyone forget that. So he blamed me for stealing everything, except for the computer and old TV that were still there: that's why he insisted it was my doing, because I knew they were crap.

There were no signs of a busted lock or anything, and about a year later the news ran a story about lock-popping and how it left no visible signs of a break-in. So my grandfather was pissed at me, and my grandmother was crying because I was going off to Asia. It was a little stressful, but I just buried it inside, figured I would drown it out later. My friend Kongo asked me what I was running from, and Lunch Box was planning on going to Iraq any day.

I got a ride to the airport with Box and told Minda I'd see her in a year or so. With that, I took off to Chicago, and after a five hour layover, I boarded a plane to Japan, a nice 12 hour flight or so. I couldn't talk to anybody on the plane, and I was in a middle seat, but lucky for me, drinks were still free on overseas flights!

I took all the crap I had dealt with and told myself, "Once I hop off this plane, I'm not going to look back." I also had no idea what to expect; there was a little anxiety, but more just anticipation. I got off the plane with two bottles of Jack and two cartons of Marlboro Reds.

I was in Japan for an hour, long enough to know that the people there were very weird. The Ramen noodles on the plane should have made that obvious, but who am I to judge? I got to Seoul, and I was met by the recruiter, who tossed me on a bus and gave me directions for when I got off. It was a six hour bus ride to Daegu, and I got to ride next to some old lady, who kept looking at me like I was going to snatch her purse and rape her grandchild.

I got off the bus, and standing there was my new boss: a short lady and her husband, a tall man, and their youngest son, who spoke

English. I was to stay at their home for two nights before moving into my apartment. Once I arrived at their home, I was given a quick examination about my history, and they asked all kinds of questions that made no sense.

Then the big question: "You are Judah, yes? From Bible! I think you people are very smart and honorable."

Yeah, just when I thought I could escape religion, it smacked me in the face. On day one, I was given the tour of government offices and doing the things that were needed to get my Korean work permit. Then I met the teacher I was replacing, who informed me not to trust the old lady, but the old man was honest and cool. I should have asked him a few more questions, but figured how hard could it be? I was used to being broke, and I didn't mind being out of contact with my family.

Chapter 19
Teach-ah, Teach-ah!

Well, the first few days were a blur, just mass confusion. I figured out the principal of the school, who knew every word in the English language, but had no clue how to structure a sentence. I had to speak to her like I would a 3 year-old, because that's kind of how she spoke to me. The male boss was cool: he only knew about 50 words, but he knew how to use them, and his hand gestures and body language allowed us to have epic conversations, and he told me some great jokes. Every day, he practiced English for at least an hour, before he called me into the smoker's lounge (the boy's bathroom).

At 9 in the morning, I had a class of adults who worked at the company next door, at 11 I had to travel to the juvenile prison to teach for two hours, and then from 3 to 7 or 4 to 9, depending on the day, I was back at the school. It was a private school, more of a tutoring service that all Korean kids did if they didn't excel in school. They brought great shame upon their family name, but I didn't buy that load of crap, and neither should you. The occasional kid took it serious, but most of them were afraid of the beat-down that would come if they screwed up, since Korean mothers all do the "dragging the kid by his ears and then slapping them upside the head when they talk back" thing.

After about a month, I got one of my better teenage students to show me how to get downtown. In exchange, I bought him some dried squid and a Coke. I also had four female teachers, all Korean, that were constantly trying to have conversations with me over drinks. Not a problem, but one of them tried to take me home. I avoided that one, but she helped me get a cell phone.

Oh yeah, and the fact that all of them thought they could speak English, but none of them could, was just nerve racking. I had to drink to dumb myself down just so that I could understand the what, who, why, where, or when part of any question they asked me. I convinced them I was deaf in one ear, so if they wanted to talk to me, they should speak slowly and facing me, so I could read their lips. Koreans are also scared of people with disabilities, for fear of it spreading.

One night at the convenience store next to my apartment (which was just a room with a refrigerator, bed, very old TV, and a VCR), I found this stuff that looked like water, but was cheaper. It was called soju. It was the Korean version of sake. I pulled a couple of bottles not knowing what to expect, until I awoke the next day with this awful feeling, like I had just been hit by a car.

I went into my class of adults, looked at them, they looked at me, and I said, "Soju, huh?" They laughed, "Oh teach-ah, you drink soju! We go out some time and drink together! We stayed out late drinking last night, too!" Their enthusiasm was endearing, but kind of annoying. Since this was the most they had spoken since I had been teaching them, I figured to Hell with this stupid book that has situations that never happen in life.

"Let's talk about last night." That got everybody awake, so they proceeded to tell me about drinking with their boss, until someone got loaded and challenged the boss to a duel (all the kids were pointing and laughing at William). I offered them my tales of excess drinking in Montreal, which turned into a question and answer session on how to order drinks in French. I told them if worse comes to worse, pretend you can't talk, and just start pointing rapidly at what you want. They laughed and said that would never fly in Korea. I said, "That always works trust me. I'll prove it tonight." So we went out to the Korean version of Hooters, and I proved it works.

Other than that, the spoiled brats I taught were learning to memorize English words, and I had to force them to learn to read by phonics. It wasn't an easy task fighting the Korean method of learning, but fighting the man is not a sometimes thing: it's an all the time thing. It's like a nervous tick: you can't control it, you can only hope to contain it.

My boss was an idiot and had no way of telling me anything without her son. Over at the prison, I was wearing a Nike jacket, and the kids were kind of sizing me up. One of them spoke well enough to understand me and translate. Most of the time, we just talked. One of the kids asked me how much I paid for the jacket. I had to get my rep up if I was going to get anything across, so I told them, "Nothing, it fell off the truck."

They were perplexed. I had to repeat, "It fell off the truck," and I had to draw a diagram on the board. They finally put 5 and 8 together, and got 20. After that I was the cool teacher: my class went from seven kids to 30 little thugs. Everybody wanted to know just how gangsta I was, so I played them some NWA, and when one of the punks said I should be in jail with them, I flipped my chair at him.

I called him out and informed him I was smart enough not to get caught. "What did you do? Oh, you broke the lock off of a locker at a spa and got arrested with $50! Don't think I'm anything like you!" Soon they asked me if I would smuggle in some cigarettes. Now, I thought long and hard about this: I could lose my job, but if I was in jail, I would want someone to be cool.

They gave me cash, and I explained if they get caught with them, I would blame them for stealing my smokes. They agreed, and one kid ratted me out, and I called him a liar. The guard strapped him to the metal bars, arms hanging up, and left him there for a day. Now that my rep was intact, I asked the kids where to go out, and one of them gave me directions to a place where his brother worked. I held onto it for a while.

I finally met some people who went downtown with me and showed me the ropes. Pretty soon, I was a regular at the English teachers' bars, and, one day, me and a student, Daniel, were walking around downtown and passed by a club called "Club Monkey". I told him, "Let's go check it out."

He was worried they wouldn't let him in; I told him to just follow my lead. The bouncer let me in right away, but held him back. I explained he was my interpreter, and he was American, and I slipped the bouncer a 10-spot. Good enough: I got in, and he got in, and we did some drinking. I saw these two blondes sitting by the bar. I figured what the hell, I walked up and started hitting on both of them. After about three minutes, they were yapping in Russian, and I played my ace in the hole: my grandmother was from Lithuania. It worked, so well that they miraculously started speaking English and I got some digits. My student was impressed, the bartender was in awe, and the American soldiers from the nearby base decided to honor my courage with a few rounds.

I went home that night, and I got a call from them the next day, asking me to go for coffee. I did, and they were claiming to be students, but I found out later they were prostitutes. No worries. We were out walking by this club that one of my thug students said to hit up, because his brother worked there. I started to walk in there when the girls grabbed me, and said we couldn't go in there, because it was mafia, and they don't let outsiders in.

I walked up like a pimp and told the bouncer who I was. He called somebody on the radio and then escorted me to a table in the back with the ladies. A few minutes later, a man walked up to me and sat down, looked me over, then looked at the girls.

Then he spoke, "How is my brother? You take care of him, yes? You take this money, give to him." Then he ordered some drinks and sardines and said, "Your money no good here, come in whenever. You are always welcome. These girls are welcome to work in the back room, if they want."

They looked at me and said, "Can you stay, and next time bring our other roommates?" I was like, "Yeah, sure," and then I proceeded to drink with the criminal element of Korea. Remember me telling you about places in the world where you are judged solely on the amount of alcohol you can drink? Let's just say, I was judged highly favorably once again, and that nobody would even think of harassing me.

I left that night with the two girls. They paid for the cab, saw my place, and laughed. They said they would clean it up, I told them they didn't have to. They tried to give me money, and I was like, "No, that's okay." I went to bed, they crashed over, it was just like old times.

I woke up, went to work, came home, and they had multiplied by three, and we went back to the club. Now Asians love blondes, so they demanded a high price, and I wasn't even trying to play pimp. The weekend came, and they said we were going shopping. Walking through the mall, one of them grabbed a white fur coat and put it on me.

I laughed, then they bought it. I took it as a thank you, and started walking the streets of downtown with all six of them, and hitting random clubs up on the weekend. Wearing a white fur coat like it was going out of style, nobody dared to question my sense of fashion. Something about my walk told people I wasn't much of a follower and, yes, I was the leader of my pack.

All was well until some Russian dude spotted me with them. After some yelling and screaming, he politely asked me to take him to the bar where the girls had been working. I did, and he said he would do security for me, and whenever I needed anything, just to ask for Vlad at this number. I was in and out of the pimp game in less than a month, but I still had the coat, and I realized I could do whatever the hell I wanted to here.

After a while, my adult students started asking me to give them free classes at the business bars. I figured, "Why not?" So we just got drunk three or four nights a week and talked about anything that came up. On the weekends, I was downtown staying at the saunas, because it was like five bucks, and you got your own little spot on the floor. The showers were nicer than my own, plus the hot tubs were nice, as long as they weren't overcrowded.

During the week, I was having food delivered from the restaurant down the street. It cost like $4 for a three-course meal on real plates, which they would pick up later. Now the meals for me were strange, because the menu wasn't in English, and the people at the restaurant just gave me whatever they felt like. I learned the names of some food, but for the most part, unless I had a craving for something, I let them surprise me.

There was a movie rental place down the street that let me rent videos; the problem was they only had a small selection of VHS. I lucked out when I found the movie "Road House". This was my typical early evening: Road House and a good, cheap meal. Then I discovered the internet café, at 50 cents an hour. There was a good three hours of playing Diablo II, and it was there I discovered MySpace, both of which filled my downtime and allowed me to meet random English-speaking people.

I found a fried chicken joint at the Casaba. One problem I figured out was that Koreans didn't really waste any part of the chicken, and like hell they knew how to quarter chicken. Leave it to Asian societies to learn how to ruin fried chicken! Now the pizza joint had a picture menu, and they weren't bad, except they don't know how to make a simple cheese pizza, or a pepperoni for that matter. Surprisingly, the sweet potato and mayo pizza wasn't that bad, if you were in the mood for something exotic.

I soon found some other Americans in Korea on MySpace, and we would waste our free time, at work or off work, posting crap on it. After a while, my routine was set, and I figured out that life needed a little more excitement. That's when it happened. I was on my lunch break across the street from my school, and I went to buy a Coke at the 7-11. I saw an American dude, and we started talking for a minute and decided to meet up for drinks later. He brought this girl Allison with him, and she was cool, I guess. She had a Midwestern accent, and we all hated the little brats in our classes. Not really much else, except we decided to shoot the shit and sing karaoke, which is the national past time of Asian people everywhere.

The next day, I saw her and was like, "We should do that again sometime," talking about all three of us. She took it to be me asking her out. So we met up, and when dude didn't show, I thought, "Well, what the hell?" We found a place to eat and drink, and on the way home we stopped at a karaoke room and sang a bit. Then we walked back to her place, and I wound up crashing there.

The next day, she offered to come by my place, and the next thing I knew, we started dating. She was Korean, but was brought up in America. I told her the only reason I was with her was because she spoke English. She told me the only reason she was with me was because I had the largest penis in the area, as Koreans aren't exactly endowed. I was like, "Okay, whatever."

Me and these girls I was talking to on MySpace decided to meet up in Seoul. I made my way up there by train and met them at the station. We had never met before, but I was sitting at the station with a boom box, playing Guns and Roses for all the world to hear. One walked up with a bottle of Jack, and her friend Nicole had a Diet Coke. We were waiting for another friend who had a spare room for the night, so we started drinking. Since we didn't have any cups, we did it the old fashion way: a swig of Jack and then a sip of Cola. I decided to rock the area with a little Foreigner, followed up by Afro Man, which I had borrowed from the internet.

Now when the cop came up to me to tell me I couldn't drink in public and to turn down the music, I looked at him and said, "No habla engles. Atah midabar evret?" (Spanish: I don't speak English; Hebrew: do you speak Hebrew?) He was very confused and walked away with haste. Then we kept drinking until the bottle was done, and the dude showed up with a key and photo directions to his place. We took off on foot, and somewhere in the process, we found our way to a rather nice one bedroom apartment.

We passed out at 11 in the morning. They had a Jeff sandwich, and I woke up next to beautiful women. Life was grand, if do say so myself. We decided to go hit this place called "Geckos on the Terrace", it's rather notorious. It's the place in Seoul that ex-patriots go to hook up with other English-speakers. While dudes kept hitting on them, they were forced to buy me drinks as well, and I hit the barkeep with a request for flaming Dr. Peppers. Now the girls were down for that, since it's a man's drink. I'll never forget the bartenders face when I set all three drinks on fire. This turned a lot of heads, since, well, we drank close to five or six of these rather comforting beverages.

This took us to another level, and we went out to a karaoke room. I did my best Clapton and Bon Jovi. The other two dudes who were macking on my dates got intimidated and tried to get me to beat it. Then one of the ladies whispered, "Don't worry, you're going home with us."

At this point, I figured I would play a game of chicken with them, and I told one of the girls I wanted to go get my nipples pierced. Why, I don't know, but it worked: the two dudes were going to have a case of the blue balls in a few minutes, because they just couldn't hang with that. So we ditched the dudes and went to the tattoo shop across the street, and I let them pick out the rings.

I passed out after the second one; it hurt like hell, but well worth it. On the way home, one of the ladies proceeded to give the cab driver a show by taking her shirt off. I'll leave that story there. The next day, hung over as all hell, we all went back to Geckos. Somehow, in the mass chaos of another day of binge drinking, we got separated, and my cell phone died. Whoops.

So sitting on the terrace, a girl comes up to me, and informs me that the two girls I was with had left. I said, "I know. She said it was okay, I could hang out with her and her friend." All was well, we went to some clubs, and I requested the DJ play "Jump Around". This was the only song I could dance to, and jumping is hella fun. I did what needed to be done that night, and woke up the next morning with two different girls, and a sore back. Now I wasn't too sure what happened to the girls in the middle stage, but I reckon I got confused and just hit on two other chicks. We swapped numbers, and I got ahold of the original girls, who were still at the apartment with my bag and most of my cash.

We decided to meet back at the Terrace, and there I found some other English teachers from my town who had an extra train ticket, so I got free ride home. All in all, a good day! I got home late, and I noticed someone had thrown a trash can and a brick through my window. The window was above my bed. I was tired, drunk, and didn't want to screw with any of this crap. So I grabbed a change of clothes and knocked on Allison's door, and she told me I could crash there.

One thing led to another, and in the middle of sex, my phone started ringing, so I got up and answered it. It was the girl who picked me up the second night in Seoul, and she wanted to have dinner the next night, so I made a date and then went back to bed. In the morning, Allison whispered that she was pissed at me and was the one who trashed my place. I gave her the key and told her that it was to be spotless when I got back that night.

To her credit it was, and I was back after dinner with my new friends who wanted to check out my pad. They laughed at the size, and when I told them the story, I got a look like, "Don't piss her off anymore." This was pretty much how things were going: life was a nonstop party, I felt like a pimp.

One day Allison told me, while we were walking down the street to her place, my fly was down. I whipped out my junk and kept walking. I went into the store to buy some beer and cigarettes, placed my junk on the counter, and the dude behind the counter was just unsure about his life at that point. I gave him the money, and he waved me off, told me not needed. I walked out, and damned if my boss and his wife weren't walking by! I introduced them to Allison, who was trying to cover my junk.

The next day at work, the boss called me into the office to explain to me Korean women are very different than Americans. I stopped him and told him that she was American and was teaching English, and he was all like, "Oh, that's okay. My wife was worried. You have a good time. It's good you have girlfriend."

I suppose things were weird for her, because I didn't want to be boyfriend-girlfriend, and I kept reminding her I was only with her until something better came along. She said I had embarrassed her by rocking out with my cock out, and to stop coming over drunk. Now look, I had my nipples pierced, and that gave me a new level of arrogance, because it hurt like hell and scared most people. I didn't have anything to prove to anybody: I could do whatever I wanted. Confidence is a dangerous thing.

I figured, "Okay, no problem. I'll give her some time to cool down." Wouldn't you know it: I lost my cell phone for the third time! I didn't know her number, so we just kind of stopped talking. I cooled off on the partying for a while, but my fellow teachers wanted to go out with me. When they found out I broke up with the other girl, my exploits had become known around the office in the "shock and awe" kind of way.

So in the classes, the middle school kids were a pain in my neck. The prisoners were the highlight of my day. One day, one of my middle school kids caught me on the elevator and, out of nowhere, I hear, "Today, me, teach-ah, two hair," and he pointed to his unit. "You, teach-ah, very hairy! I bet you many hairs!" I got off the elevator, rather unsure of the meaning of life. This really had no point I just thought it was funny.

So anyways, I got a package from my mother in the office: it was underwear and some Passover food, as this was coming up. One day, while wandering around town, I discovered an Arab market. I walked in, and, to my surprise, all the food was kosher. Shocked the hell out of me. So while shopping in the store, I see another Jewish guy, and we decided to do the whole Passover dinner thing together. We had a good time, and I found some kosher-for-Passover wine in a grocery store.

A few days later, I was walking downtown with my boss, and he took me into an herbal medicine and tea shop. He wanted to know about Jewish customs, and I explained to him that this would take a while. I began doing my best to explain things, in a watered down dialect of English I had created. Lacking any structure, more or less talking like a 3 year-old toddler. He invited me over for a traditional holiday meal with his extended family, and there he proceeded to give me strange foods, like octopus that hadn't been cooked and different stuff. All the kids were watching me, so I manned up and ate it. Later, another teacher came by and rescued me. She was supposed to be there all night, but decided to leave me hanging for a while.

We went to a restaurant, and she ordered me some soup, which I later found out was dog. The Koreans traditionally ate this to improve their sex drive. I was sick for a week. Now, I came to admire some of the Korean people, the ones that stuck to their heritage, the mountain men Buddhists that were loyal. When you see some elderly lady in her 60s bent over walking, because she had spent her whole life picking vegetables, you gain respect for those who honored the old ways.

The rest of those fuckers needed their heads examined. The rest were making me ill. They were very hospitable, but they had no notion of the power of individual thought. That meant walking down the streets and seeing fake purses and fake designers, like NIEK, PUNA, ADIOS, or FUBE. I went ballistic when a guy told me he would make me an Armani suit. How the hell could it be Armani if he made it?! It never occurred to anyone to ask, "Why this, not that?" That bothered me. Even if I was just a drunk, I was still capable of having original ideas, or at least trying new things.

115

I once used the example in my adult class where I had drawn three cows on the board and said, "One was over here eating grass. The other one is over here eating the fence. Which one is crazy?" They said the one eating the fence. I said, "What if the third cow is eating the fence as well? Does that mean that the cow eating the grass is crazy?" I got my message across that, sometimes, you have to go against social norms.

All the debauchery was catching up to me, as I walked past a bakery and saw the ex. She had put on a lot of weight: either she was pregnant, or just got really depressed when we broke up. Around this time, I saw another American girl walking by and ignored my drinking class for a minute, so I could ask her if she needed any help around here. She said, "How did you know I speak English?" I told her I lived around the corner and had never seen her before.

We kept things friendly and hung out. I showed her the pubs and bars, and the night I took her to the Club Monkey, my student Daniel was inside dancing with some college girls. I was so proud. It also happened to be French maid night, so for some reason there were close to 400 Korean girls dressed up like French maids, a sight I still can't get over.

Now we had a good time making fun of the little Asian kids walking around, attempting to talk gangsta. As far as the women went, I called it quits for a while. I was content with just hanging out. I was tired of all the drama associated with them.

I found out about this mud festival somewhere in Korea, and I met my friend Nicole there. We had a blast, walking around the beach covered in mud. They had a mud wrestling pit there, and as luck would have it, I became the intergender mud wrestling champion by taking on any female brave enough. One girl grabbed my junk, so I choked her out, and then some fat chick fell on me. I broke my rib during the battle royal, but no worries: I slapped the figure-four on that tub of lard and made Ric Flair proud, then I did a Jackie Fargo strut and left undefeated.

In pain, but I had a blast. Nothing getting an airbrush tattoo on my butt and some soju couldn't fix. When I returned to work a few days later, I remembered that my pay check was supposed to be higher. I asked about it, and they said we don't understand. The prison had given me a raise, but the school had kept it and then shorted me pay. They also were about two weeks late with my check.

Around this time, I hear my boy Kongo is getting married, and I couldn't handle the lies my bosses were telling me. They wanted to convince me to stay for another year, but pay me less. So I came in on a Saturday with the water works flowing, telling them my mother had a heart attack and fell down the stairs, and is in a coma. A little over the top, but they bought it: nobody would say such a thing, God forbid it should ever happen.

Believe me, I still pray for this from time to time, that it would happen. They paid me what they owed me and bought me a ticket to LA. Upon my glorious return to LAX, I made a quick stop at the Grove, got a good night with some random model who was still under the impression that my movie was coming out soon. The fact that I acted like I owned the place we went to only sealed the deal. I lucked out that one old friend was out of town, and I knew his door code.

After that, I took a bus to Oakland to hang with my cousin, and say hello to my aunt and uncle. I hung out there for about a week before catching a Greyhound back to Memphis. It was a long ride back, but fun. It let me collect my thoughts. Now me and this Mexicant guy were sipping tequila in the back, and the driver walked up to me and said you can't drink on the bus, and the Mexicant sitting next to me said, "Hey, homes, leave him alone! He's Mexican, like us," and the other Mexicants on the bus started bitching, so the driver let us be. Lunch Box picked me up at the bus station, and we made a stop at Starbucks before figuring out where to go next.

Chapter 20
WELCOME BACK

I decided to hang out over at my mother's apartment, since my friends lived within walking distance. Now Kongo was set to be married, and Box was getting serious with his girlfriend at the time. Kongo had decided to join the Army, but before he did he was getting married, so I tried to talk him out of it, telling him I had the door: if needed, I'd get the car started. Me and Box went to the wedding and sat in a small group in the back, being me, Little Romeo, and Box.

It was a by far one of the funniest weddings I'd been at, because the minister looked like Kenny Rogers, so the chicken jokes came naturally. Nothing too crazy happened afterwards, other than me and Little Romeo had made some progress on the green front. He was cool enough: I would hook him up with pills, and he would share his green, and we had a blast playing Madden all night.

One day as I was driving home, I got hit by another car. I was driving my mother's car, so I'd have to hear that banshee wail at me, probably accusing me of getting hit on purpose, and the car was towed. I went to the hospital, and the doctor said I had a minor concussion, nothing big, but I went to one of those "get your money quick" lawyers. I got a minor settlement out of the deal.

After that, I was just kind of sitting back one day, when Kongo asked me to do him a favor while he was off at boot camp: would I mind wife-sitting a little, to keep her company? I figured that was easy enough: she was always cool about hooking me up with smokes, and they had tons of video games.

One day, I decided to go to see a gastro doctor for my acid reflux, and an ultra sound later, they told me my kidney was extremely large, and I need more tests done. I went back to my primary doctor who got me a CAT scan. It revealed a tumor on my adrenal gland, which sent me to another doc. This game went on for a couple of months, then one day I was told the tumor was the size of a softball and needed to be removed.

The surgery was set, but I was freaking out. After a while, I was a regular at Romeo's pad, smoking whenever I could to take my mind off the tumor. Mountain Dew, some weed, and as many pills as I could stomach became my escape from reality. Now my mother was driving me crazy with her online research on what it was, this and that. My head was a mess; I couldn't think straight. All I knew was that the doctor doing the surgery didn't want to do it, because of the location and the size. Since I was already missing my gallbladder, appendix, and other random, useless organs, I didn't care if one more left the house. I was a little more scared of dying on the table with unfinished business, but at the same time I should have already been dead.

Around this time, I also lost all of my fillings, and most of my teeth needed to be taken out. Let's just say, my lifestyle had caught up to me. When the tumor got removed, I was relieved to hear that it wasn't malignant. My mother insisted I tell people it was cancer, so she could get sympathy, and she might get some money out of them, too. Well, it was funny, after the tumor I never saw Romeo again. I guess we had a falling out, not sure, hadn't given it a second thought since then.

I was still feeling like crap, but at least I was alive. I had two cousins about to get married, one in St. Louis, the other in Oakland. I hate weddings, but I was to be a groomsman in both, so be it. I finally got all my teeth pulled, and the dentures were in just after the first wedding. Now I tried to blend in and be social, but I was so far out of reality that I didn't quite know how to deal with people at this point. I was still smoking cigarettes and only a few people knew it. I behaved myself, for the most part. I took again to drinking a little, trying to let loose.

I did what needed to be done. I recall having a good time at the wedding, even dancing with my grandmother. Upon my return home, I got my new teeth, and my grandmother was sitting at the kitchen table when I came over to say hello. She kept asking me, "Why don't you go back to Israel? You were so much happier there, and I always thought you would be a good rabbi." In the middle of the week, she went to light her Shabbos candles, and this became a habit for her whenever I came over.

My friend Kongo found out he was going to be stationed in Louisiana, and his wife wanted me to help move and stay down there with them. I told them both I would help move and go down there, but just until he got back from training and moved in. I was planning to go back to Israel to do what my grandmother wanted me to do, because she was right: in Israel, I was happier. I had a purpose, and it felt good to be a part of something.

Upon moving to this one-horse military town, I found a job at a motel doing the night audit and relief shifts, because I knew the computer system they were using. My training took less than a week. I had to drive about 35 minutes to and from work, but it was all highway. I kept away from boozing it up too much, just a case of beer a week or so, with the occasional getting plastered on a day off.

I had to go to my cousin's wedding in Oakland. This sucked, but I was obligated to go, because he was my cousin, and, well, I liked the girl and all that stuff. I just really hate weddings, because they always reminded me of how lonely I really was on the inside. I had to arrange for a few days off and drive to Memphis to fly out, which was no problem: I told my boss I had to do another round of chemo.

I was trying to be on my best behavior and not get shit-faced, but seeing my stepmother just brought on all the "not having a father" issues. This patch of madness combined with my own family issues and a wedding on top just made me crack, and I just wanted to crawl into a bottle. Which I did. I might have embarrassed myself and my family, just little bit. I ran my mouth a bit, even picked a fight or two, while hitting on my new cousin's aunt. I acted like a total jackass, and I'm sorry about that. I just don't know how to deal with families, weddings, and relatives. All I had in life was a crappy job that let me watch HBO all night and then go back to keep my best friend's wife company in a house full of cats.

I was at a low point, yet I still found a way to be the coolest cat in that town. Some of the kids who hung out around the house nearly lost their girlfriends to me, but I knew better. It really isn't hard to be the coolest guy in a town with three taxidermists and a Wal-Mart. Small towns, plus young girls, divided by a military base equals a high STD rate, just the way it is. On this, my logic is flawless.

My hatred for Muslims was still growing, but not too much, since everybody in the town hated them as well. I would make a drive back once a month or so, to pick up pain pills from my mother, and to visit my grandmother, who once again was lighting her candles in the middle of the week. She was the inspiration for me to make my way back to Israel. I did my damnedest to save up money until Kongo returned, and I could fly to Israel.

He finally returned, I found a ticket for $400 one-way, and I booked that bastard. I was going back to Israel, wasn't sure where or how, but I was going. I called my old friend Todd and told him of my return, and he suggested his yeshiva, so I decided to make it work. For some reason, flipping the religious switch wasn't difficult for me when surrounded by similar people. For me to do this just came naturally, as it does for many people with the group mentality. Still wanting to fight the man does happen, but you don't go after the man upstairs, you stick to the man around the corner.

I'm at the airport, one-way ticket in hand, and I learn that they won't let me fly without a return ticket. I had to go from airline to airline, to find someone to sell me a one-way return ticket for under $1,800, because that was all I had. I finally found a lady named Sylvia to help me. She was worried, because I was very suspicious-sounding. I explained the whole deal to her: I was going because my grandmother wanted it, and if she had ever been there, she would know why I don't want to come back. She said she had been there and understood, and got me a refundable ticket.

So I got onboard the plane to Israel with about $120 dollars, which meant I didn't have the money to pay for the excess baggage. So there in the airport, I had to dump 25 pounds worth of stuff I was bringing with me. Yeah, I finally made it to the gate and aboard the plane, and arrived back in the Holy Land.

Chapter 21
My Triumphant Return to the Holy Land

Upon my arrival back into Israel, I got to play the "who is your father" question game with airport officials, but this time it was different. When they asked me in Hebrew if I spoke Hebrew, I responded in Hebrew with, "I don't speak Hebrew, but I do understand a little bit." They asked me what I was doing, I told them I was going back to yeshiva, because that's what my grandmother wanted me to do, and she is very ill.

The girl behind the counter called another girl, and they spoke for a second trying to find out if I was being honest with them. Then I informed them that I also came to visit my old girlfriend who was in the hospital. I gave them the details of how she got injured and where she was. They then asked me if I planned on seeking revenge, and I told them the truth. While I would love to exterminate every last one of those evil, turd-stained, camel-fucking bastards, I would much rather see God take His vengeance, and allow me the peace of mind never to hear that filthy language being spoken to me ever again.

They laughed at my Southern drawl, when I spoke of vengeance and satisfaction. This was holding up the line, and the Arab behind me started to bitch, so I turned towards him, looked him head to toe, then told him in Hebrew he needed to learn a little patience, and that he was a female bastard with crushed testicles. I then turned back to the girls behind the desk, who stamped my passport and gave me a number to call should I ever need their help or wanted to come over for a meal in their hometown.

With that, me and my cowboy boots took the walk towards another guy wanting to check my bags, but for some reason the Arab behind me in line was causing a scene that made me laugh a little. I walked by the security dude, as he mumbled something in Hebrew that I guessed was, "What did you call him?", but I just kept walking towards the door. I even threw in a little pimp limp as I passed him.

I then got to the shuttles to go to Jerusalem, and, while I was short on cash, I heard a shuttle driver offer me a discounted fare, because he was ready to go and only needed one more rider for a full bus. I jumped onboard, gave him the directions. I had no clue where this neighborhood was, and neither did he. I finally got to where I needed to be to meet with the people at the school. They were black-hatters, and of course, I wore a blue baseball cap.

They asked me some basic questions, and then I gave them the name of two rabbis from Memphis that had known me since I was a toddler. This was the last question they asked me at the time. They told me where I was staying, and then I went to my old pal Todd's house. It was small, with him, his wife, and three kids living in a one-bedroom apartment, a little cramped, too. He loved it and began telling me about the head of the yeshiva.

About my third day there, I was suffering from the culture shock of moving from Deridder, Louisiana to Jerusalem. Now, I only knew one way to cure the home sickness, and this is something that works for me. Yeah, it requires me listening to some Hank Williams, Jr. and a bottle of cheap vodka. It was in the middle of the song "IF HEAVEN AIN'T ALOT LIKE DIXIE, I DON'T WANNA GO", that my new rabbi walked in with a jelly doughnut to welcome me to the school.

Within about a week, the story of me dropping close to my last nickel and my clothes to hop on a plane to Israel had spread, and soon people were a little shocked at my t-shirt and jeans and baseball cap attire. I was a fish out of water. I even thought about going to another yeshiva, but figured I would give this one a chance. I informed someone that if they could deal with the boots and belt buckles, I could deal with the black hats.

I then informed them that while I understood their modesty is the reason for wearing black suits, where I'm from, that's a sign of wealth, and this is what modesty looks like in America. My t-shirts are still rather legendary, and soon I realized just how little had changed since I left. I bumped into a few people who remembered me from years before, and it wasn't that they were shocked I was back: they were shocked I was still me.

Some people change on the outside, and then on the inside, but, me, I don't believe in conforming. I believe in adapting, and forcing others to change. Now look, my philosophy with the yeshiva was spot, only my questions were a little ahead. Soon I was asked what I wanted to learn, and when I mentioned the prophets, I was kind of laughed at. Then I replied with, "I know the Vilna Gaon believed that first you learn the Chumash (five books of Moses), then you learn the prophets, then you learn the other stuff." The Vilna Gaon was an 18th century Lithuanian scholar, and amongst religious Jews is considered to be one of the most influential authorities on Jewish laws.

I just wanted to find out what I had missed, and, in addition to that, it helps build a timeline for you to better relate to your people, and then, and only then, can you relate to yourself. It was one of those heated debates that was going to get me into some trouble, because I was stubborn, and I was asking to learn what they taught at seminaries (where women go to learn).

I eventually got someone to teach me some, and learn I did, but he couldn't answer all my questions. It's hard having people tell you that you can't jump ahead like that, it's not how one learns, that your question isn't relevant, and then a week later you get the answer to your questions. I tried to explain that I'm a question and answer guy, not a read and memorize guy.

I was living in a room with some younger guys, and they were fun to hang out with, going to grab pizza and Cokes. Now I was feeling like the old me: happy, not worried about much, other than a cold shower on Fridays, when the hot water always seemed to run out as soon as I hopped in the shower. I was blending in well as an outsider, being accepted by most. I would always get asked to tell my story, which made me uncomfortable, so I would tailor my stories to the audience. Most importantly, I was reconnecting with my roots, which was somewhat uncomfortable, but things felt right. This is always difficult because my roots have always been scattered, much like the Jewish people.

Then one Friday, my stomach decided to attack. It felt like my intestines were playing Twister, and its own version of yoga. It was after the Sabbath had started, and my roommates were freaking out, not sure what to do. Finally, one of them walked to the house of a rabbi and asked him what to do. He picked up the phone and called a cab, and gave them instructions to take me to the hospital.

Now, I don't expect anybody to understand the level of pain I was in, but it didn't feel good, and the Russian nurses were trying to shove a tube up my nose and into my stomach, and yelling at me for not being able to help them. Then comes, "You need surgery."

"Okay, do the surgery."

"You must pay first."

"What? Do the surgery. Send me a bill or something."

"NO surgery until you pay!"

Then they stuck me in a room with this light that was flickering on and off. If you combine that with the fact I was on morphine, you get a blur of gut-wrenching pain, passing out, and a flickering light with people yelling at you about money for the surgery, and how they must put in a catheter, because you're not peeing enough, all in a foreign language that you're only really getting one out of every three words. It felt like I was in one of those late night B-horror movies.

The only constant was the kid who came with me to the hospital, who sat with me the whole time, refusing to leave. Finally, my friend Todd came by after the Sabbath, and we tried to get medical records from the hospital in the States. That was damn near impossible, but somehow he pulled it off. After talking to some people, they got me to another hospital for the surgery.

Apparently, scar tissue had formed around my small intestines, or in medical terms, I had a bowel obstruction caused by adhesions. The surgery was done. I remember waking up, feeling a million times better. I was in a room with three people, and guess how many spoke English? After everything was done, I had visitors coming and going, people I had never met, some I had. It was nice meeting people who cared.

I was up walking around in less than two days. They finally took out the tubes, and the young girls who brought the food around were giggling, because they got to practice speaking English. I was feeling better, would go bum smokes from people on the balcony, and even do a little bit of praying and learning in the chapel.

125

About four days after the surgery, I was out of the hospital, with a prescription for aspirin. My friend Todd had paid for the first hospital bill. So I proposed cleaning his home on Fridays and the occasional babysitting to pay him back. Yes, I was getting to use my domestic goddess skillset once again.

Soon, I found out that some of my fourth or fifth cousins through marriage had married two people from my school. Yeah, I have a big family that in America wouldn't give me the time of day, but in Israel, it's a different story: fifth cousins become second cousins. I still knew families in town that had large meals on the Sabbath, and I would go and bring a friend or two. I was once again confident that I was doing the right thing, and, oh yeah, I was sitting in the top classes in my free time. While I didn't understand every word, I got the drift enough to call out answers when asked.

I would call my grandmother once or twice a week when babysitting for Todd, who would let me make a phone call or two. Thanks to Vonage, I was always happy to speak with my grandmother. My grandfather couldn't hear a word I said, but my grandmother had no problem answering the phone.

Every conversation was the same: she would say, "I'm glad you are happy. I'm proud of you! Whatever you do, don't marry a damn Yankee! It was the biggest mistake I ever made." She loved my grandfather, just hated his attitude, and, of course, there was the notion back in her day that when you got married, you stayed married.

I stayed in contact with my friends back home, too. One of them was going off to Iraq any day, and I was waiting for the other one to get back from Iraq. Now, I don't have many close friends, but the ones I do have are the best friends a man could ask for, and they have been there for me when I needed them, and I hope I have been there for them when needed.

On occasion, I would grab a beer with a few guys to blow off steam, but since going into town or the touristy parts was kind of forbidden, we would go to the corner store and then the park, or just right there on the corner. One day, an important rabbi was passing through giving a speech, and while everyone was rushing up to him, I kind of stayed back, but the crowd forced me face to face with him. Dressed in my traditional garb of t-shirt and jeans, I got introduced. Me being from Memphis, he asked me if I knew this rabbi, and I said he prepared me for my bar mitzvah, in return I had to cut his grass. And then he asked if I knew another rabbi, and when I told him I've known him all my life, the head of the yeshiva looked at me funny, and then there were the family questions again.

I explained that I was from one of the original Jewish families in Memphis, back when they only allowed a few Jewish families in each city, in the late 1800s. This got me a good hand shake and put me in a class of my own there. Since people from out of town knew the same people I did, I'm not sure I can tell you I was once again the most popular cat in town. Whenever someone had a question and I answered it with the right question, the head of the yeshiva would stare at me and nod a bit. He would then ask me a question I should not have known the answer to, and I replied with the "this is what I reckon this rabbi would say" card. It then became a race to see if the rabbi actually said that or if I was bullshitting. As kids were racing through books, I was batting in the .700s.

If I didn't know or was lost, I wasn't afraid to ask questions of anybody. I launched great debates with random minds and pushed others to learn harder, to prove me wrong, only to come back with a book and show me what this person said and that I was on the right track. I was getting a little arrogant, much like in university, when I would show up to a lecture without books, pens, paper, just my butt in a chair was all I needed.

Then one day, I called home and found out my grandmother had pneumonia and was going to be put on a respirator to give her lungs some help. I informed my mother to tell everyone else, that once she goes on any machine, taking her off is murder. That was Friday night. I told the head of the yeshiva after services on Saturday, that I found out she had taken a turn for the worse. I started making calls to the rabbi in Memphis, who was out of town, and then I started making plans to get back.

Later that night, I found out she was on life support, and the family was going to get together to make a decision on what to do. I told a few rabbis what was going on, then I went to my apartment. I got a knock from a rabbi, who said to come with him. We went to the chief rabbinic authority in Jerusalem's home, and got a sit down with him. He ruled that nothing could be done but keep her on all of her medicine and all the life support.

He asked me who the rabbi in Memphis was, so I told him the name of the rabbi of her congregation, and the rabbi in charge of the Va'ad (kind of the local head authority), but I also informed him that he was out of town. That rabbi assured me that he would take care of it. It wasn't until afterward when I was told who that rabbi was, and that I shouldn't worry so much, because it was an honor that he saw us at all.

That Sunday, I booked a ticket to fly back first thing Monday morning. I also got a call from the head rabbi of my school, who asked me what was going on. I told him what I knew, and he told me to get on a flight that night. I told him I was leaving at five in the morning. He gave me his blessing, to go back and try to keep her alive. That next day, I was flying back with a purpose.

Chapter 22
Fending Off The Vultures

Now understand: according to Jewish law, you cannot do anything to speed up death for somebody. You cannot remove them from life support, withhold nourishment, or in any other way allow somebody to die. Allowing one to die is tantamount to murder. This was the position of my rabbi, and the position of his rabbi, and so on, and so forth. Whatever you might think of my relationship with God, my grandmother's life was God's, and only God's, to take: not the doctors, not the rabbi's, not my grandfather's, and not any human's.

The idea of killing somebody is one thing that, while it crossed my mind, is not something I would consider doing, unless it was to save a life. In fact, Judaic law goes so far as to say that if you know someone is going to kill you at 7 am, you are required to get up at 6 and kill that person first. These laws were all I could think about while on the plane back to America. When I landed, I was fully prepared to speak with the rabbi; in fact, I prepared to fight him if he were to suggest otherwise.

I arrived and went to the hospital where my family was gathered, with the exception of my brother, who was to arrive in a day or two. I wanted to speak with the head rabbi of the city, but he was out of town. Neither did I see the rabbi of my grandmother's congregation. I did, however, speak with my eldest uncle. He informed me that he knew what the rabbis in Israel would say, but the family had decided to accept whatever decision the rabbi of her congregation came to.

Now, my other uncle and my aunts all seemed to support this solution. I can't speak for them. I knew my mother held the position that she should stay on life support. My cousins were in town, the whole family was together. I went to see her, and it wasn't an easy sight, but neither was seeing my grandfather at her bedside. I was privy to a meeting with the children of my grandmother, and they were under the opinion that, according to her rabbi, it may be possible to take her off life support.

At this point, I realized they were going to kill her. There was nothing I could say, because of the rabbi's "wait and see" approach was that of there being a loophole in the Law. A real rabbi would have given a firm answer of "NO." This so-called rabbi of her congregation has no business playing God. Yeah, it's true, my grandparents weren't exactly the most religious people on Earth, but that has no meaning in determining life or death. I have a gut feeling that had she been wealthy, the rabbi might have come to a different conclusion.

There is no case-by-case decision: brain-dead or not, she was being kept alive by machines. So according to God's laws, taking her off or withholding any medicine, doing anything that would result in her death, is murder. Now, it would be easy to call my grieving family members murderers at the time, except they didn't kill her, nor did the doctors. When a person becomes a rabbi of a congregation, he takes it upon himself to lead them as his flock. This means he takes on responsibility for their behavior, much like the owner of a dog. It means that, ultimately, the buck stops with him.

That means he has to answer to God for his crime of murder. The chief rabbi of Jerusalem said he would take care of it, and his position was life, as God's Law states. So either the chief rabbi lied about taking care of it, or maybe the so-called rabbi in Memphis ignored his opinion. Or maybe, he just made the wrong decision, in which case, if he were to make this decision again, he would be a serial killer.

Yeah, his ruling in this matter makes me question any decision he made, and all of his teachings. His teachers taught him that the responsibility to protect her life was his, and he allowed her to die. He murdered a sweet old lady, who though maybe she wasn't the most learned Jewish grandmother, she still did her job in this world and will be rewarded in the next.

Who am I to speak such words, given my past? Nobody, except I do know that those who don't know aren't held responsible, and those who know are. If you know better and you're not in your right frame of mind (i.e. your loved one is dying), you perhaps aren't held responsible for the wrong decision. But since the family passed the decision to her rabbi, that makes him the responsible party. He should be held accountable, and at that point in time, I decided to confront him when I next saw him.

Not at the funeral, because that would be wrong, preferably when he came by to console the family. Well, he came by once and avoided me like the plague, and I realized he wasn't worthy of my forgiveness. In fact, his congregation should know they are following a murderer. On that day, I vowed not to step foot into his synagogue nor to forgive myself for allowing her death.

Yes, my honor was offended, and if you have learned nothing thus far in reading of my life, I have very little honor to offend. Therefore, I shall seek my vengeance. I realize I should probably allow God to take His own vengeance, but those who have the power to right wrongs and choose to ignore them are cowards in my book. Those who don't have the power to right wrongs, but still attempt to right them, are courageous in my book. Now those who regardless of their power or strength to right the wrongs give everything they have to right the wrongs are heroes, even if they fail in their efforts. They are still men of honor and courage and should be sought out and supported.

I had failed to save my grandmother's life, and I felt the burden of her death more than I let on. I had nowhere to point my wrath, except towards myself. I soon felt like a coward for the first time in my life. I felt that I let the one person who always believed that I was capable of more in life and motivated me to be a better man was dead, and I killed her. To this day, I still stay awake at night crying myself to sleep, while trying to find a way to right the great injustice that Rabbi Shai Finkelstein caused when he murdered my grandmother. Yes, sometimes I even crawl into a bottle when thinking about it.

Now understand, my grandmother was my direct link to my faith, and when she died, I had nowhere to go for that link. It was said that the purest form of a mitzvah (God's commandments) is the mitzvah done for the sake of the mitzvah. It's not for Heaven's sake, not for the benefit of anybody, but when someone performs a deed for the sake of the deed, without thoughts of reward, honor, or prestige, but just for the simple sake of doing it and being conscious of doing it. I was fortunate to witness my grandmother lighting her Shabbos candles for no other reason than to light them for the Sabbath.

Nobody was around. She looked outside. It was almost dark. And she lit her candles and said her prayers. I happened to walk in the room and noticed what she was doing. Despite it being a Tuesday, I was not going to deprive her of that mitzvah. I didn't have the heart to do such a thing. It is said that whenever you perform a mitzvah, you are actually bringing the spirit of Heaven into this world. I believe that I witnessed this, and that was the day I decided to return to Israel and seek out God.

It took me a while to do this, as I was dedicating all of my learning up to her death to her, for her sake. Every morning, I made it clear in my thoughts that any and all of my studies were for her. So yes, I take her murder very personally, and on a spiritual level, I haven't been the same since, for that matter. I haven't known much happiness, joy, love, whatever you call it, since her murder. The songs don't affect me; the movies don't entertain me.

Alone to myself, I had nothing left in the tank. I was just coasting through this ride called life, and I knew I couldn't live like that much longer. My brother gave a beautiful speech at her funeral. The murderer, who called himself a rabbi, spoke as if he knew her, which infuriated me. It was raining as we buried her.

At this point, I put my emotions in check. I reclaimed my zombie-like nature without telling anybody. I knew deep down I was a coward, and like a coward, I was going to run away from the problem. Upon returning to my grandparents' home, it seemed all of their possessions were disappearing or being claimed. It was as if he was dead as well, and, yes, he appeared as if he died that day.

I stayed with him for about a month afterwards and noticed all he did was eat, sleep, and watch TV. It was as if he had no purpose in life anymore. He put his house on the market and planned to move down to Florida, to leave behind everything he and she had worked together to build. All of their possessions were meaningless to him, while all the other family members appeared to be bickering over what they wanted.

I was disgusted, with some of them less than others, but most of them made me sick to my stomach to the point that I wanted nothing to do with them, with Memphis, with anybody. I decided I wanted to run, and where better than Jerusalem? I would become a citizen and never look back at what felt like hell. After the mourning period was finished, I packed all I could, talked to as many people as I could, to say good bye. I had no more desire to be a part of any of that crap. My friends were off fighting wars, and I was fighting a battle in my own tormented soul, that almost felt like I was destined to lose. Once again, I found myself wandering through life, alone and confused, and begging God to take the pain away.

Chapter 23
Honoring the Fallen

I returned to Jerusalem, and right away it didn't feel right. But I put on my happy face and tried. I moved from one apartment to another one, with a Persian guy, who will be known as the Iranian Bandit.

Shockingly, the Iranian Bandit was born in Iran, and then escaped by a four-wheeler ride in the middle of the night to Pakistan. From there, he made his way to Italy, and from there to New York. Me and Bandit had been in a few classes and talked a little. He had a low self-esteem, for whatever reason. Now me, I gave the appearance of having a high self-esteem, but really I felt like crap.

I had to move to the apartment that was farthest from everybody, because I felt like a coward for not standing up and doing whatever had to be done to allow my grandmother to pass naturally. Bandit had a computer and some DVDs, and we both loved a good movie to pass the time.

I also managed to get a job umpiring softball. This was kind of stressful at first, but eventually I relaxed and told the guys the truth: it's just softball, relax. I used the "safety-first" method, namely that pitches had to come across the plate between the shoulders and the belt (mainly because I didn't want a ball bouncing up and hitting me in the family jewels). After a few games, people got me, I was consistent, and every now and then after the game, some of the guys would ask to hit a little. I figured it was cool. I had nothing better to do at the time.

I still felt like shit. Whether people knew it or not, I took the blame for my grandmother's death harsh, and I was wishing I had not wasted so much time chasing women and money. After one game in particular, one of the pitchers was harassing me about the zone being hard to hit. I knew baseball, I knew softball, and I wasn't going to let some 18 year-old snob tell me anything. I told him to toss me a few, and the first one I took to the top of the short right field fence. The next three pitches I sent dead-center to the warning track. The last two I put just over the third baseman's head, in a spot that was nearly impossible to catch, where even I could have legged out a double.

Immediately, I was asked to stop umpiring and to start playing for a team. I told them, "No thanks, I'm too old for that stuff. My body might give out at any minute." After the games, I would grab a brew or two on the way home, and I became good friends with the groundskeeper. We started hanging out, smoking some hash or grabbing the occasional oxi. I wasn't trying to be innocent about anything, I was just trying to escape.

When I would go to the yeshiva, I had a harder time seeing the head rabbi, because I didn't want him to know I was a coward. I had never backed down from a fight, and the most important one in my life, I gave up in the first round. I would still get learning done, mostly in my chair in front of my apartment with a cup of coffee and a cigarette. This somehow took my mind off things, but I still had to talk them out with people.

My philosophy had the same end results, just my logic methods never made sense to others. I tried to explain that I learn better not when reading and memorizing, but with conversation and stories, or just a voice to put with the words. Because I couldn't bear the voice in my own head, sometimes I would have a conversation with somebody who wasn't there, but whom I knew what their reply was going to be.

This worked well, and Dan was a God-send when I needed company, whether just going out for pizza or falafel. We talked about random stuff, girls, the occasional getting of a phone number (not to call, just to show it could be done). I was still doing everything I could to hide my pain and put on the happy-go-lucky face. Understand, I was extremely popular: my exploits were well-known, whether it was wearing shorts to class on a hot day, or just being honest with people, or the fact people liked my accent.

Now, I was all about praying and looking for God, but my heart wasn't in it, neither was my mind. I wasn't comfortable with myself. From time to time, babysitting was a relief for me: children, for some reason, allowed me to be myself, joke around, play stuff that I did when I was a kid.

None of this seemed to matter. I felt like I was growing maturity-wise, but at the same time I was constantly feeling the urge to run amuck. I lived my life in a fashion that put me in a world of hurt physically, emotionally, spiritually, and mentally. Around this time I was filling out the paper work to become a citizen, and, well, I was also coming to grips with the fact I would be alone for the rest of life, because I was scared of being heartbroken again. I didn't need millions of dollars to be happy, I just needed purpose, and I looked and looked and kept coming up empty. I learned some places I didn't need to look again.

For some reason, the government was requiring a whole lot of paper work, but I found out if I did it from the States, it would be less of a hassle. Well, I had one friend just get back from Iraq and another just shipped off, and somehow I convinced myself and others to let me fly back to do this, only telling a few my true intentions. So I flew on a plane through Jordan, which was kind of funny, if you don't mind being surrounded by Arabs. I figured it would be a safer flight, since they rarely blow up their own people.

In the meantime, I had gotten a private sit-down with the head of the school. We talked, I tried to explain my family background, which was difficult, and he gave me a few one-liners. We began finishing each other's sentences. I explained to him why I liked country music, as it was the kind of music that helped me cope with all the stuff going on in my life and my past.

I was ready to go back and my plan was to fly to Jordan, then to St. Louis, followed by driving to Memphis for a week or two, then going back down to Deridder for a short spell, then to Florida to check in on my grandfather, and then to Seattle for a week or so to say goodbye to my brother and nieces. I would then fly to New York, stay with a good rabbi for a couple of days, and then catch a return to Jerusalem to live out the rest of my days.

Now, the stuff was going to be weird, trying to keep the faith, do all the paper work, say goodbye, and not let anybody know my true plans. It kept coming to me in my dreams, that I was to be sitting on a beach in Tel Aviv, with my baja and bottle, waiting for answers to come to me.

Chapter 24
Adios, Suckers

As I departed Israel for Jordan, I was interrogated a little harsher than I was used to, but no worries. I departed late at night, and arrived rather later. This airport in Amman was by far the smallest, nastiest thing I had ever seen. I was in transit, with a flight leaving in eight hours, so they made me leave the airport and go to a hotel, free of charge of course.

This hotel was okay; I had worked in worse. No sooner than I go to the room and barricaded it did I discover their TV had rabbit ears, and like hell I was going to sleep in this place! I turned on the TV and twisted the antennas something fierce like out of my childhood, and wouldn't you know, they had "Teenage Mutant Ninja Turtles: The Secret of the Ooze" on the old boob tube! I was unable to find anything else in English, but I watched four hours of Arabic-dubbed "Dallas".

That was until I discovered the ultimate entertainment: yes, Jordanian MTV. It had some amazing music videos, but the women were blotted out. See, a lot of Muslims get bent out of shape if you even see a woman without a veil, much less one in a rap video grinding on some homeboy talking about ice on his balls. I couldn't help but enjoy the show.

The time came for the shuttle to take me back to the airport. This nasty airport was worse looking in the day than at night, and when I got off the shuttle, some guy runs up, grabs my bags, and tells me I'm a VIP, follow him. He pushed through the crowd like an Ethiopian in line for rice. He took my bag and threw it through the X-ray screening machine, and then pushed me through the metal detector, which went off because of my belt buckle, and he just kept pushing me. Nobody stopped me, then I got in the outgoing passport line, and he just grabbed my arm and tossed me on the escalator.

I got up to the gate, and it's like a giant ash tray. The duty free store looked more like a 7-11 than anything else. So this guy stuck his hand out and demanded I pay him for expedited service. I told him I was broke, and he needed to find an American with money. He started telling me about his damn kids and how they will starve because of me, which apparently happens with every Arab businessman. They must be terrible at making money.

I was like, "Thank you, Lord, there is justice in this world after all. Let him and his whole family die of scurvy!" I got on the plane, and I'm sitting next to this fat Muslim pig from Chicago that wouldn't stop sweating or talking to me. Right after take off, I went to the back of the plane and asked if I could sit back there, and the flight attendant just looked confused but finally agreed to let me sit by myself.

I then discovered that I was one of two Americans on board, and, on top of that, the Scotch on board wasn't going to be touched by anybody else but me and this minister from San Diego. Well, we went for the gold and started hitting the bottle, and since those people don't drink and they had no idea what to do with the bottle, I just took it and went at it.

All those filthy people on board, I felt the need to scrub myself with bleach, and since I had none, I was going to drink and contemplate hijacking a plane full of Arabs. By the time the food came, I felt odd getting the kosher meal on a plane full of people who want to kill me, but I was half-way through a bottle of Johnny Walker Black Label, so that took the sting out.

I landed without any real incident, aside from me calling the flight attendant a camel jockey with a hard on for little goats, after being told I couldn't have any more to drink because we were landing soon. I got off in Chicago, and the TSA agents were going through everybody on the flights' stuff, when I came staggering up.

They asked, "Why are you coming from Jordan?"

"Well, somebody had to liberate the goats they were molesting."

The hefty TSA chick looked offended, and then I said, "Look, don't believe me, look at that one right there: he's sweating like pig, because I told him if he touched that goat again, I was going to cut off his nuts."

She started laughing and asked me if I was serious. I told her, "My friends call me Tennessee."

She told me to get out of there, then I hopped a short flight to St. Louis, where I was greeted by Lunch Box and American Cigarette, Kongo's wife at the time. We got some beers that night, then I went to piss on the Arch. After spending two days in Memphis, it was time to get the hell out of Dodge. I got down to Florida and hung with my grandfather, and did some paper work to claim my right to citizenship in Israel.

He was just wasting his days, watching the Weather Channel and going out to eat. I got him to take me to the beach a couple of times. Each time, it rained, but it was well worth the effort: it appeared the fresh air was doing him some good.

I got to Louisiana eventually, to do the wife-sitting thing. The two local kids had scored some green and wanted me to join them, but I pushed it off for a while. Meanwhile, one of the cats coughed up a fur ball and choked to death. I buried him in the back yard, put up a cross on the grave and called it a day. You were a good boy, Darkie.

About a week later, I was drunk and mouthed off at one of the kids' girlfriend, and I'll be damned if she didn't try to rape me. Lucky for me, I had enough virtue left in me to throw her in a cold shower and lock myself in my room.

I finally made my way to Seattle, where my brother had a busy two weeks, so I got to help him out a little and do some more paper work. I got to run around a hotel, looking for the things that were supposed to be on the truck. It was a huge wedding, and I had to supervise a BBQ earlier in the day. I recall the day started at 7 am, and ended the next day around 9 in the morning or so. I hung out with Jorge a bit, we tossed down a few beers, and it was all, "Via con Dios, amigo." I also got to see my nieces, who knew me as Crazy Uncle Jeffrey, a name I've always tried to live up to.

One of them didn't know me yet, and when we sat down to eat dinner, she turned her chair around, so she would have to look at me. Not once, twice, or even three times, but like six or seven. On my second to last day there, I was sitting in his office when a couple of day laborers walked in to help wash dishes. She saw them, looked at me, came running to me, and with the sweetest voice said, "Hold me, Uncle Jeffrey, I'm scared!" I got a kick out of that.

I went to Costco, bought some oatmeal, Cliff bars, and Coffee Mate, then I flew to New York. I had to wait for my passport to come back with a visa in it. My aunt got it in the mail and shipped it overnight to me. The day before I left, I found out my passport was at the main Post Office branch in the hood, as my aunt put the wrong ZIP code on it. A friend of Todd's had come by to ask me to bring some mail to him, at which point I told him the situation, and he lent me his BMW to go grab it.

I managed to get the passport, and everything was all squared. The rabbi I was staying with had a big grin on his face, because he was jealous I was going to Jerusalem and had no plans on returning. They had some speeches at the airport for new immigrants, as it was a group flight. I heard them, and when I got on the plane and sat next to some folks my age, we got to talking and got to drinking. A few beers into the flight, I just helped myself to the beer compartment in the galley. I snuck a bottle of wine for the lady, and we made it a party.

Eventually, this lady came around, asking for me, getting all my information, and she asked if I wanted to change my name. I said, "Hell yeah! Call me 'Yehuda Dovid Tennessee'."

She said, "What does Tennessee mean?"

I told her, "I might be Californian by birth, but I'm a Tennessean by the grace of God!"

Another lady translated more accurately, saying, "He is proud of his American heritage."

But Mr. Tennessee was anointed as the guy everybody on the plane should meet that day. I was fortunate enough to be sitting next to a guy who lived in my neighborhood in Jerusalem, and a girl who I would meet again. Landing early in the morning, there was a big celebration. The prime minster was shaking hands, and someone told him my name. He looked me over, and asked, "Why?" in English.

I told him, "Had there been one more Tennessean at the Alamo, there would be no need to remember it. I'm just here to help and do my part." He laughed, then some camera guy came by and started asking me questions.

I did all the official stuff and got back later, after flying all day. I saw all this stuff in my room, and I started cussing and screaming at the Iranian Bandit. I was like, "Whoever this dude is, he better not disrespect the blue shag carpet I stole from the dumpster!" Then I crashed, all jet-lagged, half-drunk, with a new name and a new attitude.

Chapter 25
They Call Me Tennessee

There I am, passed out on my bed, in my room, in the middle of a dream about something totally radical, and I hear some commotion coming from the other side of the room. I opened one eye and saw a guy in a suit.

"Joe, what the hell are you doing here?"

"Klit, is that you?"

"Yeah, 3-6 representing."

"I'm late for my mom's wedding. We'll talk later."

"Bandit, get your Iranian butt in here!"

Joe said, "What, you know him?"

"Yeah, he's my brother from another mother."

"Really?"

"Go get me some falafel with humus, tahini, and pickles."

"No chips, laffa, or pita?"

"Pita, no chips and no salad."

"Why? It's good with salad."

"I'm up, you Zionist pig."

"You want to go to shuk (the market)?"

With that, I got up and smacked the Iranian Bandit upside the head, with affection. So we started walking, and I heard, "YO! Tennessee, wait up!" It was the groundskeeper from the softball field.

"Hey, do you want to coach little league?"

"Yeah, sure, buddy."

"You do know how to coach, don't you?"

"Are you kidding me? I'm Tennessee, what do you think?"

"Give me a shout later, I'll get you the details. Later bro."

"No worries, dawg."

Then me and Bandit made it to the quickie shop on the corner. I went in, grabbed a beer and a pack of smokes, and popped a squat on the bike rack. This wasn't quite the way I planned on waking up, but what the hell?

We sat up there for a while, drinking beer and catching up, while making fun of some crazy chicks from the halfway house above the shop. Then we grabbed some grub, and proceeded to plot a course straight to Hell. Later that night, Joe came back, the question of how we knew each other on his mind. That's when the words "13" and "1" came out simultaneously. See, we had some hash back in the day, and a pipe just for smoking it. We didn't mix it, we took it straight for damn near 14 days or until we finished it all.

Then we reminisced on the gangsta pimping tactics in the Old City, where we chilled back in the day. I recalled him asking me to go with him on a pickup one day and sitting in a room full of Russians with Uzis pointed at us was a short, fat guy with machete and a trash bag. Yeah, we were kind of the OGs in the square the first time I was in Israel.

So he had sobered up: no more roofies for our personal use while smoking hash and pounding Polish Butterflies. A Polish Butterfly is a unique combination of vodka and blue Curacao, and makes your poop turn blue, and leaves you with one hell of a hangover. Well, he was still down with a few drinks, so we hit up the no-no spot for the kids in yeshiva, that being Ben Yehuda Street. This was like destiny, I guessed, that the two of us met up and were sharing a room for a few weeks.

While getting all my citizenship stuff squared away, the guy who was in charge of the learning program for us, not the head honcho, but a short English man, was giving me all kinds of Hell. I was about to tell him to shove it, but I just did what I had to do. I got permission from the head rabbi to coach the little kids playing baseball two nights a week, and he thought it was a good idea, for my exercise and relaxation. I was really teaching kids how to play a simple game, and it was actually fun. The progress the kids made gave me a level of satisfaction, from knowing I did something worthwhile.

Sitting in class one day, in a full room, I started to get double-vision, not really sure what was going on. I got up, lay down on the floor, and closed my eyes. This, apparently, was disrespectful. The teacher made some smartass comment about maybe I should teach the class. So I started to teach, from my back on the floor, with my eyes closed, and he got upset and told me I needed an attitude adjustment. So I left, went out, bought some sun glasses, then hit the bus station to catch a bus to the beach.

Now, sitting on the beach in Tel Aviv next to the American embassy was a bar called "Mike's Place". They played blues music and had a happy hour special that made the day better. That night, we hung out a bit in Tel Aviv, and then came back to Jerusalem. I got yelled at for not doing anything else that day. I apologized for the disrespect, but I really was seeing double in that room.

A few days later in another room, the same short rabbi started jumping on me for not wearing tzitzits (a four corner garment with strings attached, tied in knots, so as to remind you of the 613 commandments). He kept on about it, so I told him that it was hot wearing that in Israel, so I put them on and took them off as I could stand it. He kept at it, until an elder rabbi, who also learned in that room but wasn't affiliated with the school, stood up and told him to calm down.

This infuriated the short English rabbi, and he explained to the older rabbi in Hebrew the problem. At this point, the elder rabbi put his hands on my shoulders and said in Hebrew, "He doesn't need tzitzits. He is holy! If he needs to wear them, then he will," at which point the short rabbi told me not to come back until I was wearing tzitzits. I walked out, told my friend Todd what was going on, and tried to explain I was under a lot of stress at the present moment. I don't think he understood the gravity of the situation.

I went to a doctor to find out about the double-vision. He sent me for a CAT scan and then to an eye doctor. I wasn't sure what was going on, and Joe was heading back to America, so we agreed to meet on the flipside. Around that time, I met a guy who delivered hamburgers, and also sold hash. I decided to self-medicate to get rid of the stress.

I bought a finger or two and found a spot away from the world to smoke and relax. I felt better, the stress was relieved (success!). I started hanging out at this coffee shop during breaks and trying to avoid the angry dwarf rabbi. This is where I would work on my own philosophy, in regards to religion and life.

It was my way of relaxing and growing as a person, and for this the angry dwarf set the hounds out looking for me. I wasn't having it anymore: the more he harassed me, the more I drank. Around this time, he told me the school had two new students and to choose my new roommate wisely, because one of them would get on my nerves.

I painted the bare walls of my room with a mural, half graffiti, half political statement. It read: "Welcome to Hell, Death to America, and England, too." That night, the Lowlander came in the room and said he going to move in soon. We talked, and he asked if I cared if he smoked. I said not at all, so I lit up a cigarette, he lit up a spliff, then we swapped, and went out for a bottle of arak (a nasty tasting alcoholic beverage, but when frozen was tolerable).

I told him he could bunk in my room. The next day, this idiot from New York walks in and acts like he owns the place. He moved into Bandit's room, and, while I tried to keep my door shut, this dude never shut up, and he kept bragging about Brooklyn. If you asked him what time it was, he would give you the time in New York. If you mentioned the word pizza in his presence, you would get a lecture on how pizza is supposed to be made like they do back in Brooklyn, and not like the pizza found in Israel. When I made a cup of coffee, I got to hear all about the fabulous tea bags he brought with him.

I tried being nice, but he took over the small common room with all of his junk, and then he had the nerve to mention that me smoking outside bothered him, because when I came back in I smelled like smoke. I just told him to shut up, or I would smoke inside. That night, I took him out to a club that I normally would never go near, because it wasn't my scene, but I figured he would get his ass kicked inside. Instead, he eluded the ass-kicking by getting booted from the place for harassing the first girl he saw.

At this point, I just started hanging out on my hammock on the front porch, or on the bike rack in front of the quickie mart, just to get away from his ass. The New Yorker didn't care about anything, but his father had money, so he got away with whatever he wanted to. That just brought back emotions dealing with my grandmother, so while I

145

wouldn't kick his ass, I did my best to scare the everloving crap out of him at every turn.

That's when I just flat-out crawled into a bottle, or into a nice hash daze, and laid out on my hammock, listening to some Hank, Willie, Waylon, or Axel. The girl living next door begged me to keep the music down, so I obliged her for a week, until she came back and asked me if that American ever shut up? Me, Bandit, and the Lowlander in unison replied, "No." She then asked me to turn the music back on, up loud, with some reggae in the mix, if I could find any.

I introduced a few folks to a reggae-jazz bar called "Slow Emotion". It was a dim dive lounge right next to the laundry mat, and my apartment was about five minutes away. It was out of the way, so no one would come looking for us, and it was so remote that if you didn't know about it, you would never even go down that street. I started going out every night to avoid the conflict, mixing up the trips out for drinks and smokes with jaunts for coffee or ice cream.

The short guy would wake me in the morning, and yell at me for not going to pray. Yeah, forget about the other three people in the apartment, just me, and that's when my head would start hurting, and then my eyes. By now, I had started learning with another guy instead of the angry English gnome, and it really was a good fit for me, and the learning went really well.

Suddenly, my grandfather discovered a cancer in his eye. I had enough problems with the angry Brit with a Napoleon complex, but he kept on harassing me about this and that, and it just made me drink and toke up and wonder, "Why the hell did I come back here?" I should have gone to the government housing until I could find a job.

Then one day, I did my best to speak to the head rabbi, but he was busy, so I called the rabbi underneath him, but he was busy, too. I just worked myself up into a frenzy, and it had been building up for a while. I couldn't take it; I didn't know what to do. I went back to my room and started grabbing everything Jewish that I owned, no matter how sacred, no matter how expensive, and just said, "Fuck it."

I put it in a shopping kart along with some newspaper, and then I grabbed some lighter fluid, cologne, and aftershave, and dowsed it all. I lit a cigarette, tossed the match in the cart, and sat on my throne, watching it burn, giving it all back to God. I made my own sacrifice. I broke all the bonds I had with the Lord that day.

Now I understand, Bandit, not knowing what to do, grabbed the neighbor and ran out with water, trying to put the fire out. I went inside, grabbed some clothes and some food, and walked out, not sure where I was heading. I found a tree with a nice, old chair underneath it, and sat down in the shade. Listening to some tunes, I felt liberated. At the same time, I knew what I just did was going to get me a direct flight to Hell and/or the Looney Bin.

Some people I knew saw me and started talking to me, saying, "Jeff, how could you? Jeff, what the hell? You're going to burn for this."

I stood up and said, "The name is Tennessee, and I'm already in Hell! It can't get any worse!"

Chapter 26
Fire on the Mountain, Run, Boys, Run

I was taken to the hospital, to see just how crazy I was. Now I'm a little fuzzy on details, but I went to the hospital, and the doctors were confused why I set the fire. I tried to explain that I was tired of the mental anguish, the stress, the utter chaos of people trying to tell me what to do, and that I wasn't a drunk or drug addict, I was just trying to cope.

They didn't quite get that. What they did somehow get was that God spoke to me and told me to set the fire. That was not the case, but the broken language barrier with the double-vision led them to send me to a psych ward in the middle of nowhere. The doctors there put 2 and 2 together and figured out that I was just really stressed, and that was just a blown gasket. Since I didn't try to hurt anyone or myself, I wasn't a danger, and while my method of fire might seem strange, it's not like throwing it in a trashcan would have been any different. It was just the first idea that popped into my head.

They asked me, why just my Jewish stuff? I told them I was just trying to break free, I guess. I felt like, somehow, this would sever my ties, with the stress of struggling between religion and my past transgressions. It was a rational decision, just an irrational action, with unknown consequences. The straw just broke the camel's back. I snapped, but I was coming around. I realized how messed up it was, but it wasn't like I could just take it all back. The doc at the psych ward was like, "Go away somewhere for the weekend and relax."

So a friend took me into his home, but problems arose when I realized what I had done, and I started to go into kind of a shock, and then went back to the hospital. This wasn't a bad thing, because I ran into somebody that helped me put things in perspective.

This guy worked at the quickie mart where I would buy beer and squat on the bike rack. He never really said much to me, but I saw him outside smoking, so I bummed a light from him, and he wanted to know why I was in the hospital. I told him stress; I had just snapped. I told him my struggle. He told me he had cancer and to look at him, he wasn't worried. I bit the hook and asked him why?

He said, "Do you want to know what the secret to a happy life is? I'll tell you. Just remember, the only person you have to answer to is God, and nobody else. Not the rabbis, not your friends, not your parents, just you and God. If you can live with yourself, so can God. Don't worry about the other things. I know you, you're a popular guy, everybody likes you, they tell me you're outside drinking, having a good time, talking. Nobody complains about you.

"If you ever need help, ask me. I have connections. I'll take care of everything. Keep your head on straight. Me, I'm dying, and I don't have a worry in the world, except for my family. That is why they are here with me. You be strong and don't take any shit from anybody. You don't answer to them. You answer to God and yourself. Remember this, and share it with your family one day."

Then we parted ways, and I felt better, a lot better. I went back to my friend's home, and he took me back in. When I left on Monday, he gave me a spare rooster. This rooster had a purpose: when I went back to my old apartment and put him under that annoying guy's bed, the next day around 10 in the morning, he pissed his pants.

I had moved in with my friend Todd, and I stayed my distance from the school. They wanted a letter from a therapist to see if I was nuts. I would do some learning and take my rooster for a walk. I talked to the therapist, and, yeah, he didn't understand my methods, but he understood the stress and pressure I felt. He recommended I take a break, maybe get a job, get my mind off the crap and pressures of the life I was living. He said I didn't appear to be an alcoholic or a drug addict, but he could see how it might be that I would develop dependency issues, and I should probably lay off drinking my troubles away.

Chapter 27
It's Burger Time

With that, I went down to Tel Aviv with the idea of just being a simple cook. Something simple, nothing complicated like being a rabbi or whatever. Just doing something easy in the place I wanted to call home. I saw a place that was hiring, asked about it, and was told to come back tomorrow. Now, everybody in town told me the guy who owned this burger joint was a jerk. He openly admitted to being a former crackhead and a disbarred attorney.

I figured what the hell, and I started working for him the next day, at around noon. There were five people in the room: one had the job, the other four were fucked. Let the best man win. I did what I had to, and at 7 pm, he asked, "Who is going to work tonight?"

Nobody else said anything, so I said, "Fuck it, I will." It was a slow night, but a few people were coming by. I had to do prep, grill, deep fry, serve drinks, waiter, bus boy, and cashier. I did what I had to do, and by the end of the night, the place was a mess. Grease was everywhere, the product of poor ventilation mixed with wind, and me being out of the swing of things and freaking tired.

By 5 am, the boss was ready to close. The place was still a mess, and I had been cutting my hands all night on the stainless steel counters and vents, which had not been smoothed. That meant thin cuts, and I would get more just wiping down the counters. I told the owner I would come back at 10 and finish the job, and he said fine.

When he walked in the next morning, he flipped out, started yelling and screaming, and throwing shit around. I was like, "Chill out, I got this," and started scrubbing, spraying, scraping, sweeping, and mopping. I did this for hours, and, by 4 pm, I was done. I went back to my place and showered, figured I was probably fired, but at least I went for it.

Around 5:30, I got a call asking where everything had been stocked the day before, when we had five people trying to find room for everything. I came in, looked for stuff, and found it, knowing I was going to get blamed for it being in a place not intended to house whatever it was. After a quick dinner of Ramen noodles and a Coke, I went to the bar where the owner was and asked him if it was cool if I spent some money in his place. He was pissed and started yelling again.

I said, "Dude, look at my hands!" I showed them to him, with my multiple scars, scabs, cuts, and blisters.

He asked, "What's all that from?"

I told him last night and this morning, the stainless steel, some of the chemicals, and working my ass off.

He said, "I didn't know," and let me in. He bought me a shot and told the bartenders to give me half-off. He offered me some skunk (really good weed), and then we started talking. It turned out we both had run-ins with the same gangs in different cities. I told him about getting pulled over by the heat while driving the "master's" car.

He laughed and asked how much time I served. I told him none: the guy was on the payroll. It was a test to see if I would rat or keep my cool. I told him I couldn't really do that much in the States anymore, because of political heat and my connections being under surveillance. He got it.

Now, the manager of the restaurant was a pastry chef, who was weird. He called me in, and started yelling and screaming at me. I told him, "Look, I was dead-tired, but I kept pushing. I understand you're worried about rats and stuff, but, dude, I came back. I've done this before. The dirty, greasy pans and pots I left in hot, soapy water, so that I could come back and not attract rats."

I walked him through the place and then told him to relax. I would figure out a better system for working it all solo, but it was going to take another shift for me to get it down pat. He said, "Whatever."

I went back to the bar, started drinking some more, hung out. The next day, I got a call at noon from the owner, asking me to come to the restaurant with him. I met him, took a quick walk through. He said he fired one of the other three guys last night, and he was giving this other guy a shot tonight. He asked me to show him a few things and to try to clean the place up before he opened. He paid close to 10 bucks an hour, so I took my shirt off, threw on an apron, and went to work.

151

Around 7:30, I finished and went back to the bar to get paid. I got paid, and then some kid came up to me, asking if I could get some hash for him. I asked him, "How much?" He said just enough for a couple of joints, he was going to Egypt the next day. I had some back at the hostel and hooked him up with the little I had left.

He gave me close to three times what it was worth, and it was enough for me to buy another finger, if I knew anybody that sold it in Tel Aviv. After I got back to the bar, the owner walked up to me and asked me to help him with a keg down stairs. I went down, and he asked about what I just did. I told him I sold him what I had left. No big deal, guy had paid me enough to buy some more when I find a dealer.

The owner said, "I'll make you a deal: I'll give you 12 sticks. You sell them for this price, and for every 4 you sell, you'll have two extra, to either smoke or sell." He also said he would send people to me, that he had a lot of heat on him.

I thought to myself, "Here I go again," but what the hell? I had never been busted, and worst comes to worst, I go on the run with my American passport. I still didn't speak that much Hebrew, but I was a communications specialist, so I could find a way to make this shit work. He told me he didn't really trust people that didn't speak English. I told him I didn't trust anybody anymore, but I knew who was cool to sell to. This wasn't my first rodeo, and it wouldn't be my last either.

He said, "Cool. By the way, you're working tomorrow morning. I want to try opening at noon." No problem, but I reminded him I was staying at the hostel, paying night to night, and I still had stuff in Jerusalem, so I would need to go back one day, so a schedule would be nice. He said he would talk to the manager and get it worked out.

With that, I was back in the game. He bought me a few more shots. I was drinking some beers, hitting on some chicks, the same old story, different town. The next day, I'm at work when this Swedish chick I knew from the hostel came up and gave me a big hug, and I told her I'd call her when I got off. The boss man told me his ex-wife was a Swede, and he gave me some cheap pickup lines. Then the manager showed up late, and I got to hear the boss man yell at someone else. This time the pastry chef-turned-restaurant manager and he had it out.

The dude made a schedule, and it showed that only three employees out of seven were left so far. I start prepping the food and stuff. The boss man sent me a few dudes who were looking for the "special burgers", so I hooked them up, got some extra cash, and went about my work. I hit up the hostel later that night, and after showering, I hit on the chick at the desk for a while.

When the Swede came by, we went out for coffee and stuff. I got a few art supplies and later on that week used them for some abstract art that I had made. I managed to get to Jerusalem on my day off, and I got a call as soon as I got into Jerusalem, to see if I could work that night, so I rushed back to Tel Aviv to hit the grill.

Around closing time, the owner came in and asked me what the hell I was doing there? I told him the manager called and asked me to come in. Believe it or not, he started yelling. "What the hell! I wanted you to settle all your affairs and come back in a day or two! This is bullshit! That little faggot hasn't worked a shift yet! What the hell, I'm going to fire him soon, the bastard. I'm going to get a guy in tomorrow. Can you train him? And if he can't do it, I'll find someone that can."

All was going well, and about a week later, he told me about the apartment upstairs from the bar that he owns, where the bar manager and other folks lived. I got to become one of those "other folks". It was awkward for a few days when I moved in, until we all went out a time or two. I was doing alright: I wasn't making a fortune, but I was getting by and having a blast. I spent my days walking down the beach or working. It was kind of like reliving that dream I kept having, of sitting on the beach with a bottle, watching the sunrise, wearing shorts and a baja.

Life was pretty fun. I would screw up from time to time and get yelled at, once, and it wouldn't happen again. Around this time, I started getting some Arabs coming in, because they thought I was an Arab. Now, these filthy rats were attempting to buy the "special burgers" from me, and I told them to fuck off. Then the cops came by and searched me, but they never went looking in the flour jar. Then they went to the bar and searched the Big Boss man's jacket.

The joke was on them, because the Russian strip club across the way made a point to send the bouncer over a little bit before the police came to visit me, to give me a heads-up. To show my appreciation, I went over after work to thank the bouncer, who informed me that the Russian from the quickie mart was his cousin. He told me that I needed to earn some respect in the neighborhood, soon, because he and the club were going to be gone: the police on the beach were cracking down on everything.

The owner came down one day and was arguing with somebody from the hotel, who called the health inspector out and all kinds of random crap. I just kept on trucking: he would fire and hire, and fire, and I was working close to everyday, and kept my ducks in a row. One night, these five towel-headed, goat-molesting, shit-for-brains Muslims came in and started talking that pig slop of a language know as Arabic, a language not fit for my dog to hear spoken, and one of them slapped the table.

I grabbed a wrench and knocked him upside the head. It drew a little blood, and he tried to swing back, but I was behind the counter. I leaned back, grabbed his filthy arm, and twisted it across the counter. I smacked the wrench just above the back of his elbow, and his buddies pulled him back and ran off.

I didn't make a big deal about it. The next day, the boss came down and said some of those pigs went into the bar, trying to start a fight and mess up his bar. Keep a look out. I grabbed the wrench and showed it to him; he brought an aluminum bat and put it behind the register. He asked me if I knew how to use it in a fight. I told him not to worry, I can take care of myself: if need be, I could get a gun and stay strapped, just in case. He said no, because it could come back to him, and he might get arrested. The cops had been after him for years.

Then he got curious about the gun, and asked how I could get one. I told him straight-up, "I've got a rep in Jerusalem. I was there long enough to know a few Russians, who happened to like my attitude, and the fact I'm an American who can keep his mouth shut, and I wasn't from New York or Miami."

On one free day, I got a pay check from the baseball league. I deposited it in my bank, and, the next day, said, "Aww, hell, I miss having my nipples pierced. I'll get them redone." It did hurt like hell again. I bled for a day or two, but it didn't get infected like the first time.

I was hanging out with the Swede one day at a café, and, somehow, a random guy found me attractive and started hitting on me in front of her. She looked at me and asked, "How come you didn't tell him you are not gay?" I told her about the times in America that I could remember, when random dudes would offer me money to come back with them, or just flat out ask me to go back to their place.

Flat-out, I'm not gay, and I'm comfortable enough with my own sexuality that I take it as a compliment, and not get all offended that it was a dude saying I'm hot. My boss heard me telling the story and asked why I didn't bring any girls back to the apartment. I told him I don't like crapping where I eat. Too much drama comes from that stuff. He said the Arabs are all gay, and then we swapped stories of those inbred child-molesters that enjoy beating their wives and having sex with teenage boys.

This was life: people getting hired, fired, me getting yelled at for random things. I knew I needed to step up and start experimenting in the kitchen, so I did. I started making chicken tenders and hot wings, inventing my own sauces, putting new twists on things. All was well: I got to drink a beer while flipping burgers on the beach and getting paid for it.

I went and got a tattoo of Captain Morgan on my right calf, and to show it off, I have to do the pose. Why, you ask? Because I had the bottle in my hands and figured I should remember the occasion. Plus, I had nothing better to do that day, and all the cool kids were doing it, so I figured I'd show them how it's done. Did I mention that showing the tat off gets me free shots most of the time? And it's an instant conversation starter.

I was back to a rock 'n roll lifestyle: the occasional line of coke, all the drugs I wanted I could get, plenty of beer and whiskey. What more could I ask for? The Swede left town, and I got hammered more often. Me and my roommates would go out after hours, or sometimes we would all have a night off and go out on the town or hang out in the bar. One night they ganged up on me while I was sleeping and trimmed my beard. That night I clipped a lock of her hair, and put it next to the cat named "Gangsta". She blamed him for ripping it out. I was satisfied with my work.

I had a religious customer who enjoyed his "special burgers", and we would talk God and the politics involved with yeshiva, and freak out people who didn't know I had been in yeshiva just before this. One day, the girl I was sitting with on the plane, when I made my triumphant return to Israel, was working at the bar, and we were talking about stuff, typical shop talk. She had broken up with her boyfriend. Anyway, I was getting comfortable, which meant any day now, something was bound to go very wrong.

Chapter 28
The Wall

I was on cruise control during my shift and when I was off, except that I would have to start my day by cleaning up after the stupid Israeli who was working at night and insisted on playing some awful techno. I can deal with all kinds of music, even techno, but his stuff was just horrid. I would help him expedite orders from the bar at night, not because I was paid to, but when I have to clean up after people, I try to make sure the mess isn't too bad.

All in all, things were going good, except the restaurant wasn't making any money once Israel went after the people firing mortars across the border, and the police started sending mounted patrols to the beach. Nobody was to be seen on the streets at night; some nights I wouldn't even make an order of fries, and I would be forced to close early. The strip club had closed, and Arabs were running amuck in the streets, while the police were all over my boss and me.

I wasn't selling enough hash to make any money or extra smoke. I tried running stuff to Jerusalem; I didn't tell anybody I was coming down, just hopped on a bus. When I got off, security went all up in my grill, going through my bag, they even checked my hat. I guess, for them, the appearance of checking was important, when all they had to do was pat me down: I was carrying four sticks in one pocket, two in my sock, and one more mixed in with my cigarettes.

I got the royal, "We are watching you, and we will get you one day!" speech in Hebrew and in English. I walked into the red light district in Jerusalem and sold it all in 20 minutes to three dudes from England on their gap year. I had never met them, so I took a hefty sum and left without any exchange of names or numbers. I returned to Tel Aviv, mentioned what happened, and decided all Hell was going to break loose soon.

Sure enough, my boss had hired some fat chick from England and told me to train her. I did what I could, but there wasn't much to work with. The other guy working was a guy from the bar, and he was fine. In fact, I wish I had gotten to work with him more, since he was one of my roommates. Anyways, I was getting sloppy in preparing food, forgetting a few things from time to time, extras like grilled onions or peppers. Normally this wasn't a big deal, but it happened to normally be the boss' food.

I actually made decent tips for a guy. So this guy came by, talking about his new restaurant, and he just kept talking. I told him I pretty much made everything on the menu from scratch, except the burgers (those came pre-made). I was proud of my hot sauce, my wings, all of my other sauces, and my fried chicken batter was better than that guy from Kentucky. We were talking, and it was a very slow night.

My boss came by, and I mentioned we were probably a little low on gas. I told him I didn't know anything about the gas when he hired me, but I figured, since we were open longer, the gas would run out faster. Somehow the next day we had almost run out, so he ordered some but yelled at me for not telling him ahead of time.

Then this guy showed up again, talking about his damn restaurant, and he offered me a job at it, when it opened in August. I was like, "Thanks, but I'm happy." When my boss heard, he said I should take it. I didn't think it was going to be open longer than a month: it's going to be overstaffed, prices way too high with high overhead costs, and it's out in the middle of nowhere.

Well, the next night, I was working with the new girl, running orders back and forth, also doing the register and helping with whatever. Things got interesting when a couple of Arab punks came in to order food and paid for stuff. I wasn't paying too much attention, but when the last guy tried to pay for one drink with a $100 after his buddies had ordered and paid with $100s, I told him I couldn't break it, he needed to go next door, and he left. I didn't think anything of it, until the boss counted the money at the end of the night: it turns out there were three counterfeit bills in the till.

I'm not sure if it was the Arabs, but logic tells me it was. For all I know, the girl could have just as easily taken the money in. I got yelled at like a bitch, and I got paid with the counterfeit money. I was told I had two weeks left and to pack up and get out of the apartment, but to be sure to keep on working.

I tried getting another job, but since I was a little drunk the night before the interview, the trial went shaky at first, and at the end I had some problems with the Hebrew. I tried a few other places, but the pay sucked and the pace was more than I wanted. My grandfather was sick, and I just wasn't sure how much longer I could keep up.

I worked for the next two weeks and told my roommate how to make all the dressings, batters, and marinades. I went back to Jerusalem and tried to get into a yeshiva after talking to my religious friend in Tel Aviv. For a people who want to educate and love everybody Jewish, once they heard I had kind of a nervous breakdown and I wasn't rich, they gave me the cold shoulder. I wanted nothing to do with religious people. I'd rather be with a bunch of bacon-eating Jews that drive on the Sabbath than the orthodox Jews who wouldn't help a little old lady who fell crossing the street.

I had enough of Israel: it chewed me up and spat me out. I had to get an emergency passport to leave the country, because having just become an Israeli citizen, they wouldn't let me leave on my American passport. So I got my old roommate, the Lowlander, to help me expedite the whole thing. I kept hearing my mother bitch about having to try to take care of my grandfather. The two of them never got along, and so I thought, "Well, shit, I got nothing to do until August. I can come back and work for dude when his restaurant opens. I'll at least get paid good. In the meantime, I can do some good helping my grandfather out."

This meant I was flying back to America, through Brussels, to Miami, and then up to Delray Beach. It just so happens the European Union head office is located in Brussels. My stop-over was uneventful, except for a great conversation with some French girl, and me marking my territory on every one of those pink buildings. Every end of the world scenario I've ever heard of starts with a united Europe.

I decided to mark my territory and have my own claim to fame, if arrested. I was open about it, even took a dump in front of the main lobby doors at 6 in the morning. It was light out, people were walking by, but no reaction. They just let me be. I guess they're used to that kind of thing on the Continent. I arrived in sunny, south Florida on a rainy day, but no matter: I was out of the grasp of those filthy, stinking, camel-turd chewing Muslims once again, and I had lived.

Chapter 29
A Helping Hand

Upon returning to sunny, south Florida, it was my goal to help my grandfather out some. I had to see what was going on, due to the mixed reports I was hearing from my mother and her twin sister. I got back to God's Waiting Room and discovered my grandfather was actually in better spirits than when I had left. He had moved into a two bedroom condo about five minutes from my aunt, he had advanced from the Weather Channel to the classic movie channel, and he was due to start physical therapy for his hands. About two or three days later, he received orders to be placed on oxygen.

Not surprising, since he had his first cigarette at age 9, and when he was in the Navy at the age of 16 cigarettes were a part of his daily rations. His hearing had been mostly gone for years, but we understood each other: blame it on years of bluffing each other in Gin. On a side note, knocking in Gin is for sissies. We had many a game waiting on the same cards.

His physical therapist, a nice lady named Robin, said she might be able to find me a little work. Now at this point, I gave Joe a call, since he lived up the road in Fort Liqourdale, and I had a couple of Cuban cigars on hand. We partook of the sights and tossed back a couple of rum runners in coconut monkey heads, on the beach, while smoking those fine, hand-rolled stogies.

Soon, I found the Starbucks nearby, and after a while, I got to know some regulars the way I always do. Anyways, between food and therapy, my grandfather spent most of his time on the computer playing Solitaire or sleeping in his chair. I was soon asked to help some guy with a bad back do therapy at his home, in his pool. His daughter called and asked me how much? I told her $15-20 an hour. She said, "How about $40?"

I said okay and showed up the next day. The old guy was cool, and I pretty much just had to walk him around the pool for an hour, or help him to practice treading water. So an hour in the sun got me $40 two to three times a week. The rest of the time, I would hang out at the Starbucks with what I dubbed "the Starbucks Mafia".

We had a bookie, a nice guy with access to an internet gambling site in Costa Rica and connections in Chicago. We also had a slum lord with a good-looking daughter, who was just a little too young for me but nice to look at. We had a Jewish lawyer, who had three clients and a wife who was in her 20s. There was the cougar, who was living off her ex-husband's alimony and her own net worth.

Then there was me, Tennessee, a guy who enjoyed a little cough syrup in his coffee, fresh out of the pool, a little Seagrams 7 in the Pike's Place brew. Everybody around knew my cough syrup in the coffee wasn't top-shelf, but it wasn't bottom-rung, so from time to time we switched up brands and all pitched in for a bottle.

We would sit around for a good two or three hours, talking sports, money, alcohol, business, drugs, and women. I was hooked up with random work by the lady who had the boutique next door. She would ask if I could fix her satellite radio or her computers from time to time. I would receive margaritas in exchange for my hard work.

Once again, life made sense, basking in the sunshine, with a little bit of random conversations on life, love, and, of course, the occasional joint. I was back to living outside the law, with my access to random cash poker games in the back room of a bar within walking distance of my grandfather's condo. Now, this bar was 21 and up only, and it was by far the biggest redneck joint in a 250-mile radius. It was a dive, with $2 drafts and a weird collection of old people.

I was having a good time. Most days, I would go over to my aunt's to watch TV and smoke cigarettes, or hit the bar up and talk to the 90 year-old guy with terminal lung cancer smoking through his tracheotomy. He was cool as hell, doing shots of Jack and chain-smoking filterless Camels, and he had no problems grabbing any piece of tail that walked by him. "Just reach out and grab," he would say. "What's the worst thing that could happen? I'll be dead in a month."

Me and him understood that we really had nothing to fear but death, and both of us had come to grips with our lives, so the notion of death didn't scare us. My days with my grandfather, though, didn't see

162

much action, outside of driving to Costco for muffins, or going out for the early bird special somewhere. I enjoyed the time, but really wasn't doing way too much, as he was okay living by himself. We had plans to go to Chicago for a cousin's wedding, and I still had that job in Israel I could snag, but figured it really wasn't a big deal: I could do whatever I wanted.

Me and the Mafia were cool with each other, enough to gossip about all the extremely rich people walking around us, to the point that we would play "pass the cougar". What is that, you may ask? It's where you make stupid passes at hot older chicks, just to see how big an asshole you can be and still get laid.

The grass was green enough on that side to make me think I needed to just stay where I was for as long as possible. Now, one day, during a vigorous win for me in a round of "pass the cougar", I chanced to look out the window and see my cougar's husband pulling into the driveway. Using all my magic ninja skills of evasion, I had to climb out the window of a 30-foot balcony, work my way down to the ground, and make a run for the gate. After telling that tale, I was given the elite status of the craziest SOB to ever run the gauntlet of that Starbucks, which entitled me to, well, nothing, outside of free coffee, and access to a couple of random jobs.

Most were legit, some weren't. One in particular, somebody had keyed a car, and it would cost more to repair the paint job than the car was worth. I was told to send the kid who did it a message, which really wasn't that hard. When I found him, I twisted his arm and made him lick all the bird poop off a statue in the park across the street. It was also funny, because the kid was one of those small penis, wife-beating, swine-molesting Muslims who threatened me with jihad, after I called Mohammed nothing more than flying carpet thief, who would rob caravans, and, for sport, cut the heads off people who complained. Apparently, he thought it was my car he was keying, so the fool decided to key a pink '56 Cadillac Coupe-Deville, because I trashed talked his prophet. It was fun, and after I did that, I really had nothing left to prove to anybody around West Palm.

My grandfather was doing good, and he let me do most of the driving, but on occasion I would let him drive. It was just good, old-fashion fun, hanging out with him on Sundays, driving up or down the coast, and grabbing the occasional bite to eat on the beach. I had found something as close to a normal life as I had known in years. Things were going good: both of my friends were back from the battlefields, I was having some fun in the sun, and when people harassed me about not having a real job, I would simply point out I was taking care of my grandfather, and that would suffice.

I didn't expect anything in return; I just felt it was the right thing to do. If that meant sacrificing a career I didn't want or need, what's the big deal? Then people would say, "Why is it that you don't care if you have money or not?" My reply was simple: I had lived my life hardcore and kind of figured I'd be dead at this point, so every day I was living on borrowed time. Plus, I had already been living like a king, and having no money or a ton of money wasn't getting in the way of that.

It was time to go to Chicago for the wedding, so we figured we'd stay in Memphis for a day or two, and then head up north to Chicago. My grandfather's health agreed with the plan, and away we went North.

Chapter 30
Chicago Done Did It

On the way up North, we stopped in Memphis to pick up my mother and kick back for a few days before my cousin's wedding. I dropped my grandfather off at my uncle's, and I went to Lunch Box's pad for a few days. His girlfriend was working her way through the police academy at the time, and he was bouncing at a strip club. We hung out a bit, talked, I got my drink on once or twice, went to the shooting range with his girlfriend, went through a couple clips. I really don't like guns. I don't mind them, but, if I'm going to kill somebody, I would rather have it be personal, like a knife or my foot.

After my short visit, we hit the road and made good time to Chicago. My mother went to sleep in the backseat, my grandfather was chilling with his oxygen tank, and I just focused on getting up the road without getting a ticket. Not sure why I was in such a hurry. OH YEAH, my mother was in the car, and I couldn't deal with her talking! We made it to Chicago, where we got to the hotel. I went for a walk and a place to buy some cigarettes, just anything to not deal with Minda.

I went to a cousin's for dinner, and the next day went to a Cub's game with my cousins. I had a few "Old Styles", the traditional beer to have at Wrigley, and had a good time with the youngsters, who were home from college. That night we went to the rehearsal dinner, and it wasn't bad at all, considering I hate weddings.

The next day, the wedding was cool, but my grandfather wasn't feeling too well, so I didn't get trashed or anything. I socialized with the family, a few guests, nothing out of line. The day we were supposed to leave, my grandfather was not really feeling any better, and my mother had a flight to catch. In talking with my cousins, I decided to get my mother to the airport, and then I called an ambulance to take my grandfather to the hospital.

After a few hours in the ER, it turns out that between the VA, his other hospital visits, and the fact that he never understood the diagnosis, he needed a valve replacement, and his oxygen levels were out of whack. I spent the night at the hospital and called the uncles with updates and stuff. The doc wanted to do surgery, and so my uncles came in for the talk with the doctor, because I didn't want to be held responsible for his wellbeing.

My grandfather asked me what I thought. I told him to wait until my uncles came in to make a decision, but the choice was his: did he want to live, or just wait to die? I could tell that without his wife, he was just waiting to die anyway. What could I tell him to do?

So he had the surgery. I started staying over at my cousin's house and going up to the hospital during the days, spending most of my time waiting for the doctors to make their rounds, and grabbing some food in the cafeteria. It was pretty good food, and on occasion I would go out for lunch. I even met a girl there, and when I stayed downtown once or twice, she stopped by after her shift was over.

My cousins were coming up just to visit. They also understood how rough it was for me, probably more than I did. After a while, I would go off for long walks, grab some food, go to some Cubs games, just to get away and clear my head. It wasn't easy seeing my grandfather so helpless and not really being able to do anything about it. He was recovering slowly, so next came the decision on where he should do his rehab at: Florida, Chicago, or Memphis?

It was decided he should go back to Memphis. The problem was we really had no place to stay. I could stay at my friend's house while he was rehabbing, but all of our stuff was in Florida. It was also determined that he should move back to Memphis permanently. It was rough to try to make decisions that I shouldn't really be having to make, and then having to be the update machine on his condition.

In total, I couldn't tell you how long I was in Chicago, but it felt like forever. My torture was taking its toll, both mental and physical. The worst part was people trying to give me praise for being a great person, for taking care of my grandfather. At the same time, I was having to use his credit card just to survive, you know, eating and stuff, and the area his hospital was located in wasn't cheap. Plus, it was really just one of those things that happened, and I really didn't plan on having to be the one doing all that stuff. I tried to be responsible, but the praise for me was harsh.

I was having a hard time helping him in and out of bed, so he could use the bathroom. I was helping, but at the same time I also felt he would probably be better off with someone trained for this stuff. Eventually, my aunt came up to fly back with him, and I was going to drive back to Memphis. Alone, no problem, it was all gravy.

So on the way back, I took my time. I stayed at a hotel, picked up a bottle that night, ordered a pizza, and tried to relax. It wasn't easy. My anxiety level was going through the roof, and about a month before we left, my whole left side had gone numb. I had gone to the hospital, and they thought maybe I had a stroke. They weren't sure. All I knew was that I wanted to get away, crawl into a hole, and never come out.

People kept saying, "It's so good that you're willing to do this," like I had a choice. I suppose I had a choice, but it really wasn't: I didn't want to take care of him, but nobody else was going to do it. I really did want my own life, but I couldn't have one, which made the praise just hurt more, because I didn't want to help at this point. I felt like, I can't do this, but I have to.

Around this time, I got back to Memphis, and my grandfather was in his rehab place. I admit it: I went to the bottle to escape the reality that had become of my life. I had nothing going on at this time positive, I was looking for a place for my grandfather to live, and my mother decided to join the band wagon. I couldn't take any of this crap.

I spent time at Starbucks and thought, "This can't be the rest of my life." I was having a tough time trying to get a grip onto the reality of what life was at this point. I wanted more, and this was all I had. My grandfather was on the mend, going to a nursing home on temporary status, before moving into an apartment. It was time for me to go back to Florida and pack up the sweet life, to head back to Memphis for good. It was like there was some kind of strange gravitational pull that always forced me back to that town I hated and loved at the same time. I loved it for what it could be, and I hated it for what it was. It was kind of like myself.

Chapter 31
Packing Up

The time came for me to go down to Florida and pack up all my stuff, and his stuff, and drive it back. I opted to rent an SUV for the week and drive it down and back up. I wasn't looking forward to any of this, but it had to be done, and nobody else would do it, so I manned up.

On the way down, I got stuck in Birmingham traffic and stopped off at the Hooters for some wings. A couple of rounds later, while talking to some people, I decided while down in Florida, I should check out the Keys. After drinking for a while, I got a second wind and kept going for quite a way, and when I had enough, I pulled into a cheap motel for the night. Early the next morning, I hit the road, and made great time while listening to the satellite radio in the car (it was better than I thought it would be).

I got into Florida and called my aunt, to let her know when I'd be in. Got in a little earlier than expected, so I grabbed a coffee with a few members of the Mafia and kicked back on the fact I'd only be around for a few more days. I went over to my aunt's and had dinner with her and her friends, and made plans to go to the beach the next day with one of her friend's granddaughters. I also got online and asked a girl I knew back in high school, who lived in the area, if she wanted to go down to the Keys for the day.

Well, I was at Starbucks with the Mafia early Saturday morning, and she called up and said, "Okay, let's go to the Keys." Alright, I figured it would be cool. In the meantime, I was headed to the beach with the granddaughter of my aunt's friend, no biggie. I was working on my tan, grabbed a bite to eat, left, went back home, stopped off at the dive bar to say hello to the old timers and what not.

All was well. Talking to some people, I decided to see if the girl from high school wanted to leave that night. Somehow I talked her into it and picked her up pretty late, I guess. She had a bottle of wine for the road. We took off and started to catch up. It turned out she was a lawyer, so I told her about some of my escapades and the LSAT score I picked up, trying not to brag, but it just happened that I mentioned that

I did get into all the schools I applied to. She asked a question about Harvard, so I mentioned I got wait-listed and eventually got in, but chose to live a life of less stress. I would have probably enjoyed it but had no real reason to go to law school. No desire.

We kept talking. It was a fun ride, watching the lightning hit the water, while driving down at night on the two lane bridge. It was a beautiful sight, if I do say myself, a natural wonder. We got down to Key West around 3 or so and started looking for a room. I eventually found one: it was like $300, something ridiculously high. Eventually we said to Hell with it, and we took the room.

The fat desk clerk was being an ass, so I figured it would be fun to mess with him. We did so, calling down every other minute for this or that, and finally he got really pissed. I loved it! I had done his job before and never with the attitude. He deserved it.

The next day started with some drinks, which led to walking around and drinking. It was a fun day, and as night came up again, she made me promise to get her back before the morning. I decided to be responsible, but one thing led to another, and she rode off on some guy's bike, while I mooned a whole crowd of people.

We made it back to the car, and then she said that she trusted me and felt safe with me. I was caught off guard. Why, I'm not sure, but I had a great time. On the drive back, we made good time, if I do say so myself. We pulled into her driveway, me driving, her sleeping. When I woke her up, she invited me to stay. Against my better judgment, I accepted; I was tired and a little tipsy, so what the hell, why not? It didn't take much for me to pass out.

So I woke up the next day, and I was headed out to pack up my grandfather's stuff, when she gave me a spare key to her place. I wasn't quite sure what that meant, and because I really didn't want to think about going back and dealing with my grandfather, I spent the rest of the day dwelling over why she gave me a key.

After I was done brooding, I went back, packed up, and then hit the Starbucks, kicking it with the Mafia. Trying to figure life out was just killing me. I decided to stick around for a couple extra days, but I'm not sure why, but I did. I spent the next few days with her and thought to myself, "Maybe this is what I want, the kind of life I should have," or something to that effect. I tried my hardest to make her think I was a jerk, but on the last day, I left her a rose and a note, expressing my deepest wishes and desires. I was rather drunk, but it still proved I was the most romantic man alive.

The next day I took off and felt crappy. I spent half the drive debating with myself what to do. I wanted her, bad. And she wasn't a drug-addled whore, or a stripper, or like my mom. I felt good with her. I tried apologizing to the girl, but kept putting my damn foot in my mouth. This is something I almost never do, but I got flustered. Oh well. Another one bites the dust.

I got back, and I was still unsure of everything. I had talked to my friend Joe in Florida, and we were joking about a BBQ on the beach. It sounded good to me, so I got a flight and hotel package near the girl. I remember her telling me that when she moved into her apartment, she lost these fancy sandals. I recalled her kicking them out the window on the way back from the Keys, because I tend to remember everything.

I called up my cousin, who is one of those fashionistas, and described them so she could help me find another pair. She told me about an outlet store that carried those, and I found one in Atlanta. I made some inquires, and when some gay guy came on the phone, well, I admit it: I flirted with the dude to get him to ship them to Florida and get me a better price. I told him they were for me, and when he said that they were ladies shoes and I needed to adjust the size, I laughed, called him silly and told him I was only 5'4", but I had the heart of a lion and stamina of a tiger.

Just to be honest, I told my grandfather I had spent too much money, but I'd find a way to pay him back. He mentioned he wanted to put me in his will, but one of my uncle's objected, and then he told me he was just going to pay me every week. This only made me feel like shit, plain and simple. This brought money into the equation, and that was just wrong.

Chapter 32
The Fall of Tennessee

I drove my friend's car to Little Rock and parked, all hopped up on Red Bull and coffee. Sitting around the airport, I couldn't figure out why I was doing this, other than to go to a BBQ on the beach with Joe and to stay away from dealing with my grandfather. I was lucky, in a way, when I bumped into the former governor of that state, who I overheard talking about going to Jerusalem.

I asked him if he would take a note for me to the Wall in Jerusalem, where the custom is to place a note with a prayer inside into the cracks in the Wall. As one pilgrim to another, he said he would. I wrote it in Hebrew, a real simple message: "What, God? Show me what to do."

Then I got called up to the gate, and they told me they were seating me in First Class. I thought to myself, "Wow, that was quick. Thanks, God!" I'm really not sure if the governor delivered the message, but I like to think he did. Things on the trip were going swell: I landed, got picked up by (my brother from another mother and a fellow fan of 3-6 Mafia, before Hustle and Flow) Joe, and then we went to town. Walking through the Ritz, I decided to put on the Ritz and walk in like I owned the place. I even tossed in the limp to go with pimp walk.

We got upstairs, grabbed a cabana, and went to town. My aunt picked up the sandals and dropped them off for me, and I went to my room and waited for the girl to come into my lair and get her damn sandals. Me and the girl wound up going to dinner that night, the next night doing a wine tasting, and the following day watching movies all day. It was a great time.

Me and Joe did some ribs, chicken, the works, on the beach. I went for a swim fully dressed, because, well, I do that type of thing when in the mood. After our fill of flesh, we took the party somewhere else and had some more fun. I was due to fly back the next day, so I did whatever needed to be done before then.

A friend of my aunt's offered to fly me back if wanted, so I could stay longer. I decided to think about it, and talked to my grandfather and my uncle. They said to wait until my grandfather got out of the hospital before I headed back to Memphis. So I was back in the swing of things for a few more days, but the girl was avoiding me, even though I was going to drive her car back to Memphis for her, because she got a new one.

I spent more time running around with the Mafia and old timers at the bar. I was given the day my grandfather was to be released, and I drove back a couple days early to get settled in. I was restless. I didn't want to spend the next 15 years taking care of my grandfather: it would be the end of my life. I didn't know what to do. My head was killing me, my side went all numb, and I went to my friend's apartment.

Sitting there, staring at the gun. I knew that wasn't the answer, so the day before my grandfather was to be released, I bought a ticket to New Zealand to clear my head. I also bought a tent, a backpack, some beef jerky, and a few random things I might need. I wasn't sure what to do next, I just knew this wasn't for me. I remember being at the cardiologist office with my grandfather, and he made a mess in the bathroom. Not like a little mess, but the kind of mess you would expect to find at roadhouse in Mexico somewhere. That took me over the edge.

I knew I couldn't do it, that I was destined for something better, and at this point, anything would have been better. It wasn't the money I owed my grandfather that I was worried about, or even the girl I had spent so much time thinking about. She tried to talk me out of going, but she wasn't going to give me a reason to stay. It was just the notion of ending up alone, battered, beaten, and having nothing but a lifetime of regret to accompany me in my years of a life to come, whatever time I had left.

I felt like I deserved better, but I couldn't make it happen. This sense of entitlement might have been a little arrogant, I know. I wasn't really planning on coming back from this last adventure: I was kind of planning on dying there before the age of 30, like so many had predicted. Yeah, over the years, I had kind of not planned on living past

30. I just figured I'd be dead by then, so anything after or before was kind of like living on borrowed time.

I wasn't really looking forward to anything, so much as just to the left and right, because, well, death never takes a swipe at you from the front or the back. He just kind of takes a swipe at you from the side, usually from your off hand. Since I don't have an offhand, I had to have my head on a swivel. I picked up a carton of cigarettes and a few lap dances on my last night in Memphis. The next day I was gone: Denver for a few hours, then LAX for another couple, and then Auckland.

Chapter 33
New Zealand

Sitting in the bar in Denver, I recalled the fact that I've been here before; not anything big, it just reminded me of the places I've been. Like that time in Atlanta, where I damn near missed my flight because I was drinking on Central Time, and the time in Denver I missed a flight because I wanted a cigarette. Some people might have a problem with this, but I didn't: things come up sometimes, and you're happier where you are than where you're going.

Now, I don't pretend that I went to New Zealand for any other purpose than to drink myself into a bottle and crawl out into something, anything better, if not just stay tucked into that bottle like a turtle. On my way off, in LA, wandering around, I came across a few guys who I'd met in Denver. We joked about the fact we had different flights all the way to Auckland, and then we sparked up a nice joint before the flight. Getting past security stoned worked well for me. Wearing my Baja and shades, the TSA agent asked where I bought it. I told him somewhere in between Memphis and Lake Charles. He laughed and said he hadn't seen anybody wearing one of those in years. I grinned and told him to dust his off: I was going to bring it back into style, one way or the other.

He asked what the other was, and my glossy eyes gave it all away, as I raised my arms and gave him a purple nurple, or nipple twister. He cracked up trying to hold back the other agents that came running up. I felt merciful, so I dropped my grip, and he asked if I was holding. I said, "Not anymore, homes." He waived me through the rest of the line.

I got to the gate, and it was packed. I walked to the bar, grabbed a drink, and started chatting up some couple on their honeymoon. After the lines thinned out, I made my way to the gate and got stuck in the middle of these two fat ladies.

After the flight took off, one of the ladies complained about my lack of respect for her size, and then I was given a seat in the rear of the plane. Talking to the flight attendants, I was drinking it up, as if we would crash any moment. It was a very turbulent flight, and I was paranoid due to the weed I had just smoked.

I eventually calmed down, and some kid asked me about how to score when we get over there. I told him, "Anywhere you go, just look for two things: long hair and a pizza parlor, and you'll find a way to get stoned." I was well aware of these cardinal rules to buying weed in foreign countries, and so felt it my duty to share with the youngster, who was taking his first trip out of the States.

After getting off the plane, customs was weird. They took some of my beef jerky, checked my tent, and were very concerned with my lack of plans. However, they let me go. I grabbed a flyer that advertised cars for under $6 a day. I called up and got one for three months, and then I stopped at a grocery store, bought shoes, a phone, and a trunk full of boxed wine, baked beans, and tuna. You can live off it, that's all I cared about. I grabbed an atlas and a full tank of gas and headed up north, to the northernmost point on the island nation.

Driving all night and sipping from the box, I finally made a pit stop and decided to camp there for the rest of the night. The next morning, I was woken up by the sounds of sheep and a cocked shotgun. I got out, and the guy said, "This is private property!" I said, "My bad, dude. I'll pack up."

He said it was cool, and asked if I had any good drugs. I told him I just got in, but then he recommended I take a hit off his already lit spliff. We had a good talk, and before he left, I gave him a shot of Jack Daniels. He asked why it was that I had several bottles on me. I gave him the answer, and he said, "That's just fucked up, man. Here, take this bud with you. Stay here as long as you want."

The next night, when I woke after a very restful slumber, I continued up north. To make it there by sunrise was going to take some time on those gravel roads. Finally, I came to a fork in the road, and the sign had been somewhat twisted. I was looking for a while, trying to make up my mind, knowing I was only few miles away but not sure left or right.

Well, since Death would most likely strike from the left, I went to face him head on. I drove for another 10 minutes, and it appeared that I was in a parking lot, but I couldn't see anything. I stopped to look at the map but no dice. I tried to back up and heard the wheels spinning, no traction. I thought to myself, "Mud or sand, either way, I'm hosed."

I got out and started looking for a nice tree branch to gain some traction, when I came across a sign that had been knocked down. It said:

Be Alert
High and Low Tide From X to X
Do not drive unless in 4-wheel drive vehicle

I was in a mid-80s Toyota Corolla. I knew damn well I would be stuck for a while. I did what I thought was right given the time of night, and the fact the radio station had a nice mix of Skynyrd and AC/DC: I popped the trunk, grabbed a box of wine, rolled up a joint, and then I laid back listening to some solid tunes, watching the stars. I realized I had nothing to fear, for in a place of such beauty, God had to be with me. I just waited for Him to send me some help and rocked out.

After the sun had risen, I saw some Korean tourists, and I asked them for a ride or a phone to call a tow truck. They looked confused, so, what the hell, I asked them in their native tongue if they cared to dance. When they said no, I told them to sit down and shut up, class was about to begin. I was close to using all my Korean speech, so I finished it up by asking them if they cared for a drink (they said no), and then I told them to enjoy their trip. I didn't speak any English to them, and while I knew about what level of English they were at just by looking at them, I figured it wasn't worth my trouble to ask them for help.

They left, and a guy came up in a makeshift camper and said, "Oh hell, I can get you out." He gave me one end of the rope, I attached it to the frame, and he began to pull. As he was pulling, he started to sink. I offered him a shot, he offered me a toke, and we sat there waiting patiently. Eventually, someone from park services came down and pulled us both out, and then he showed me how to get to where I wanted to go.

I pulled up, and it was worth the trouble: blue skies, blue seas and snow-covered mountain peaks, as far as the eyes could see. I camped out in the car, since the sign said no camping, and waited for the sun to come up the next day. I met some others with the same idea, I sold them a box of wine for some traveling cash, and we waited for the sun to come up together. Sure enough, the next day, the sun did come up again. I wasn't sure at that point whether it would or not.

Turns out, all that trouble was worth the sight before my eyes, and words would not begin to do it justice. So therefore, I recommend you put down the books about other people's lives and start living your own. Now I hit the road again, and low on gas. I decided to grab some gas, not enough money for a full tank, but, what the hell, I let the kid fill up my tank while I went to the bathroom.

Then I hopped in the car and took off. I passed by a cop with my heart pounding, with the idea of a high speed chase running through my head. I knew their police don't carry guns, so I had that going for me. But I was lucky: he didn't follow me.

As night began to fall across the land, I opted to camp on the beach despite the warnings, because, well, my name was Tennessee, and what's the worst thing that could happen? Nothing. The morning sun woke me, and the wine in my body told me I should probably drink some more. So I did, and then decided to hit the road again. See, I forgot which side of the road to drive on, but I was reminded by a line of cars as I made a turn, and eventually I had to choose between hitting a truck head-on or wrapping myself around the big, old tree in front of me.

I opted for the truck, and bounced off his headlights like a champ. I successfully kept on the road and passed the guy, who was yelling and screaming. I was alive and unharmed, so I just got on the right side of the road and kept on trucking, as "Highway to Hell" had just started playing on the radio. I was head-banging down the road for a while, until I passed a proper tavern with a motel attached.

I went in, asked about finding a place to camp for the night, and grabbed a beer. It was good, I must say. I was talking to some guy who offered the rugby field for my sleep purposes, when the owner shouts

177

out, "Where are you from?" I told the truth: "Memphis, Tennessee, home of the king and birth place of the blues," with my head held high. I noted that I was Californian by birth and Southern by the grace of God. The owner yelled back, "Give him a beer and tell him to come sit down," even though I could hear him perfectly well.

I got another beer and went over to him. As I got there, we shook hands like men sizing each other up. He asked what happened to the car, because it looked like Hell, all covered in sand, missing half the front end, and dragging a bumper from a pickup truck. We started talking, and out of the clear blue he says, "Ya know, I reckon Ronnie Van Zant was the greatest man to ever live."

Speechless. I began nodding my head, as he began reading off the list of reasons why. Now, I've heard some rather large statements in my day, but that one took the cake: to say that the barefooted lead singer of the greatest rock and roll band ever to grace God's green Earth (Lynyrd Skynyrd) was the greatest man to ever live won the contest. I wanted to argue, but thought to myself, I suppose you could say that. I wouldn't, but who am I to rain on his parade? I agreed, and then he offered me a bed in the back of the house, free of charge, and told me I was welcome to stay as long as I wanted. If need be, he would put me to work.

At this point, I went outside to actually inspect the vehicle for the first time. He followed and laughed with me, and then he said, "Don't worry, this will cheer you up," and started rolling a joint. I recall thinking to myself, "If this ain't Heaven, I'm not sure I want to go, because this place felt like home." For me, that was a big statement. I'd been wandering for years, always looking around every town I visited, wondering, "What if I lived here?"

They call it Cain's curse, destined to wander the earth, never finding a permanent home. It is said to affect those who killed somebody in a previous lifetime. I had found what I had been searching for, and it was perfect. I knew I was home that night, when I passed out on the cot set up just above the empty kegs.

Chapter 34
The Law

Awoken the next morning by the sound of a barking dog and flashing lights reflecting off the two-way mirror in the back room, I saw a cop talking to the owner, listening in the best I could. The cop was saying, "The driver of that car had hit another car and taken it onto the 90 Mile Beach, all of which violated the rental agreement. The car needed to be returned to the rental car company." The owner told the cop that he saw some black guy drop the car off last night and hop in another car.

The cop then mentioned that he was headed north to look for this other car, and if the owner saw the driver again to call him and try to stall him for a while. The owner agreed and then walked back with a look of satisfaction on his face. He gave me a map, and he said, "I'm not going to tell you what to do or how to do it, but there is a pond about two days away. There is a town another five miles past the pond, just follow the ocean. You're welcome back here anytime. I'll call the cop in about four hours and tell him to go west, while you're off to the east. Get some distance, get out of sight. Here is some cash, in case you need it. Best of luck to you."

Now I knew I had found a home. He also gave me a small quantity of the stuff we were smoking the night before, which is as good as good luck. With that, I called the radio station and requested the DJ play the theme song to the "Dukes of Hazzard" and told him to dedicate it to my 5 year-old son who was dying of testicular cancer. Not to make light of testicular cancer, but I wanted to make sure the song would be played.

Off I sped, straightening the curves, and flattening the hills as fast as I could go. I dodged the main roads, and I was on gravel for a while. I pulled up to a secluded beach that night to sleep, and awoke the next day. I continued my journey to the Lily Pad Pond, as it was called. Out of nowhere, this damn ewe and about five lambs came running across the road. I tried to swerve, but on the bright side, I only hit one. I felt bad, got out of the car, poured him a shot and one for myself, of course. Then I hopped back in and floored it.

I was running low on gas again, but really didn't want to pull up anywhere. Unfortunately, I had to. I got on a main road, pulled into the station, gave the kid $5, and got just enough gas to get me to where I was headed. Night began to fall, and I was close but couldn't find the pond: they don't believe in street lights in New Zealand.

I parked at another beach, and in the morning started driving again. A cop pulled up behind me, and I was like, "Oh well." He asked me about the car. I told him I had hit a rock on the beach and was driving it back to the car company, but couldn't drive at night. My heart was racing. He saw the wine on the seat and asked me if I was drunk. I told him that was left over from last night. He bought it, and I drove off.

I found a beach town and asked the locals for this place on my hand-drawn map. I figured it out and started off to it. About a half-mile from the road where it was located, that same cop pulled up behind me. He said, "You stole some gas at this gas station."

I told him, "Nope."

He said, "Okay, well, your car has been reported stolen by the car company, so at this point I'm going to write you a ticket to appear before the local judge on Wednesday." Then he said, "Are you drunk? I think you are. Blow in this."

I blew. Fortunately, I was just under the limit, as it goes up by your age over there. I was okay, but then the cop saw blood and wool and asked, "Did you hit a sheep?"

I was like, "That's old."

He said, "Don't talk at this point. I'm placing you under arrest. I'm going to read you your rights."

After taking my statement (which consisted of saying the sheep came out of nowhere; it was an accident), I was locked up. Well, every two hours they let you go outside for a cigarette, and Saturday night they allow you two beers with your meal. On Sunday morning, I was told that since they couldn't find the owner of the sheep, the charges would be dropped until they could find the owner. Then I would be prosecuted to the fullest extent of the law.

I realized it was too late to dump the car, as I was walking back to it. I had already been charged with grand theft auto, but released back to the car until Wednesday, when I had to appear before the judge. I went about my business, telling folk on the beach my troubles over boxed wine. They would normally just give me grass, saying it would help cheer me up. I figured if I kept this up, I might have enough to start selling and just buy another car.

All was going good, until I met an Israeli who wouldn't leave me alone, until I agreed to go back to his hostel. He said I could stay for free. Turns out, he was one of those Messianic Jews for Jesus pushers. Now, I might not be the most practical of Jews in my method of worship, and I'm not going to tell a Christian he's worshipping an idol with that cross, but a Jew for Jesus is just asking for trouble.

I did what I could not to argue scriptures with him, but he kept up until I laid down the Biblical Law by telling him to pick a religion. I didn't care which one, and I don't think God would either, but he needed to pick one or the other. He was visibly shaken by my rant, and confused enough that I gave him Siddur (a Jewish book of prayer) and told him to read the Hebrew as if the words were his own and to try to feel God's love.

The next morning, I saw him do that and start crying. I'm glad I could help him out, poor guy. I hated to leave him like that, but I had to be in court in a few days. I went about and drove to the court house a few days early. They had warm water, a luxury I hadn't used in a while. I opted to just wait in and around the car for judgment day.

All was going well until the battery died. No matter, I still had plenty of wine, beans, and tuna. I waited patiently that cold, rainy Wednesday morning, for my name to be called. Sure enough, it was. They told me I needed a lawyer, so I went outside and got one. He explained the car thing might work itself out, but the sheep was going to get at least two years if they found the owner.

I went back before the judge, and the prosecutor made a good argument to put me in jail while waiting for the owner of the sheep to come forward. However, my lawyer made the better argument, suggesting that the sheep might not have even been a sheep, it could have been anything. The judge agreed and let me go on my own recognizance, provided I handed over my passport and not to flee before my next court date.

It had been rough and cold, I hadn't eaten a warm meal in some time, but I'd be damned if I was going to prison over this. I went back to my car, with a dead battery and a smell of wine and tuna that I could only compare to the open air fish markets in Seoul. Another day went by, me still drinking and smoking in front of the court house, and a cop car pulls up. It's the chief of police.

I told him my long, sad tale, starting with taking care of my grandfather, and omitting the plan to drop the car in a pond. He told me he would call the rental car company and find out what to do about getting me back home. He then told me to hang tight, and to not trust any of the blacks in town: they might try to steal my wine. I laughed, and he said he was serious. I told him they would have to pry it from my cold, dead hands.

That night, as I was passed out rather comfortably in the back seat, I got a knock on the window. It was a female officer. She asked me to pack up my stuff and put it in her car: we were going to the chief's house. As we pulled up, I saw him carrying a cooler to his squad car, and he said to toss my gear in the back seat. Off we went, as he was taking me to the American consulate. He had already called ahead, so they were expecting my arrival in Auckland later that day.

I wasn't sure what was going on, except I would be getting a passport and flight to LA that night. I thought to myself, "It could be worse," and we had a good conversation about crime, and how it doesn't pay in his town. I kept thinking if I had two more Tennesseans, I could take over half the country in a month, and people would fall in line like the sheep. The best part is I wouldn't need a gun!

After a good hour of silence, the chief asked me if I had any clue whose sheep it was that I had hit. I told him I had no clue what it was, but where I come from, it would have been legal for me to pick it up and eat it. He started laughing and mentioned he had done that once before, and then we swapped jokes for a while. He opened the cooler filled with beer and said to have at it. We drank for a while, then grabbed some lunch.

We got to the consulate, and he wished me good luck. With that, I got my gear and went inside. The sweet lady inside gave me a bunch of paper work and told me to get a photo taken. I came back, she gave me some money, and called me a cab to the airport. I was headed back to LA, with a little under $30 and a massive hangover coming.

Chapter 35
Home Sweet Home

So arriving at LAX, I wasn't really sure where to go next. I did what anybody would do: I got one of those shuttles to the beach, and when the driver stopped and demanded payment, I gave him an expired debit card I had picked up over the years. When he went to run it, I disappeared. Blending in with the strange beach folk in Venice, I just went south. I eventually caught a ride to San Diego. I still had the boxes of wine, just in the bags that were inside the box. My load was getting lighter by the day, and, hell, the weather was great.

I wasn't really sure what to do or where to go. Being homeless has a freedom to it, but it also messes with your head when people ask where are you going. If you say, "Nowhere special," it just doesn't get you anything. You tell people a city on the other side of the country, well, that changes everything! After a couple of days in Tijuana, I rode to a rest stop in Amarillo, where I found a trucker headed to Memphis. I hopped aboard and got back to the home of the king.

That really was just the beginning. I was hanging out over at my friend's house again, but wasn't sure what to do next. I held onto my dice for a day or two before I rolled them, and then I went to tell my grandfather I'm sorry, and I would pay him back eventually. He gave me some cash to get around, and I went back to Lunch Box's. On day two, I had a sharp pain in my stomach and couldn't hold anything down. Once again, my intestines had decided to do some yoga.

So I was back in the hospital with a tube up my nose, waiting for the pain to go away. They did the surgery the next morning, and I was stuck in the hospital for another two or three weeks. Not much happened. I got released and stopped by my grandfather's afterwards to grab some clothes. He suggested I stay there. It was happening all over again, but I had nothing else to do at the moment.

I started talking to some old friends off and on. When I healed up, I started taking care of my grandfather again, taking him to the doctors and Costco. It was getting close to Christmas, and he was doing okay. We wouldn't let him drive, which made life weird, but okay. I was just doing my thing, started praying again, learning with the rabbi nearby on random days.

As Christmas came, the girl from Florida was coming up. She called me a couple of times, and eventually we went out once. She made a joke about me working for her dad, and I figured, "Sure, why not?" I met with him around New Year's Eve and made some jokes, while sipping from my flask. It went well. All I needed was a small job to get me out of the house a couple hours a day; if I could pull in close to $100 a week, it would be fine.

Well, it took a month or so before I went to work for him. He asked me to do some manual labor for a month, it paid hourly. Around the same time, my grandfather needed to get a pacemaker. Shortly after that, he was upset about the fact I was working and would leave him alone with nowhere to go. One thing led to another, and his pacemaker acted funny one weekend, so we went to the hospital. It was an overnight stay and turned out to be nothing big, just a funny feeling when it went off.

About a week later, a social worker came over to see how he was getting along. She asked me to let her know if he needed to go to assisted living. Now, I understood this would probably leave me homeless, and I shouldn't make that decision, but at the same time, it made sense. He would have a nurse on call, people to talk to, people to help him get dressed, and someone to take him wherever he wanted to go. I didn't want to send him to an assisted living home, but I also didn't want to be sponging off him.

I also had to go to the hospital for a day, as my stomach was messing with me. After spending most of the day there, I realized it was just stress. I wasn't sure what to do, and it's not like you can just ask around, "Hey, what do I do with my life now?" Sometimes in life, we have to make decisions that will put us in a position that we don't want to be in. But the decision got made, and she recommended that he go to an assisted living home, and then she told him his VA benefits may help him with the cost.

I was tangled in a web of stress and decided that maybe the bottle would help with all of this. I had a friend come visit from Australia, and we went out and about. All was okay until I finished training at the job and was about to move into my friend's mom's apartment, with no electricity and under renovations that weren't going to be restarted anytime soon. It was a Friday night, and, come Monday, I had to get out of that apartment. The more I was sitting around the apartment, the more stressed I was getting, knowing I was about to be in world of hurt. My last pay check was like $47, so I knew that job wouldn't be enough for me to turn the lights on or even pay for gas and food.

I wasn't sure what to do, and the more I sat around, the more upset I got. So I went out for a drink, and, well, to spare people the details, I drank for a while longer, switched places, and even swung by a friend's house that night. I was three sheets to the wind, but I didn't hit a tree, a car, a sheep, hell, I didn't even break a traffic law, except for the fact I was drunk, and somebody reported me in.

I didn't care all that much. I called my friend, and he tried to bail me out, but the bond didn't get set until Sunday. My date with the judge would probably be Monday. Now, I really didn't care: I was debating staying in jail. Despite the cramped cell and bad-tasting food, I found peace there. I realized I screwed up, and I'll pay the consequences. Maybe this way, by the time I was 30, I would still be alive. I wasn't sure I was actually going to get out.

A friend of mine showed up as my lawyer, which was cool. I told her I just wanted to get out of there, which I suppose I did. Now, it wasn't until I got out and found out all the money it would cost to keep from going back to jail while on probation that I realized I would have been better off in jail.

Instead, I went back to the condo of shadows and took the easy way out, by calling my family in California to borrow the money just for the courts. I had to borrow money from a lot of people to keep out of jail for that year. I do regret my actions needed for survival. I went to a couple of AA meetings, but I got to tell you, I couldn't take the people telling their stories. It was only getting me fired up, and AA made me want to go out for beer.

I wasn't going anywhere fast, and as much as I wanted help from my friends, I couldn't ask them. Hell, I really didn't want to ask anybody, I just wanted to go to jail, do my time, and move on. Somehow, one of my friends came by and picked me up one day, to spend some quality time in the AC, and I just kind of stayed there for the weekend, and that turned into a few months.

Right around this time, after months had passed, I went looking for a job, knowing I was in a world of hurt. I couldn't land any of them, because I didn't have a car, until I got an interview with a Starbucks on the other side of town. I was also making my way back into the Jewish community, as it was the holy season. I suppose it made sense in my head, even if the people whose couch I was on didn't get it. All they knew was, if given the chance to bum off people, I would. But I also had some mad housekeeping skills.

I made my way to temple one holiday and was talking with this guy most of the day, between prayer and food. Somehow, we managed to lock ourselves outside while smoking behind the kitchen area, and surrounded by a high fence. We were stuck. I tried to climb the fence, and was impressed with the fact I got up there. However, getting down wasn't going to be easy, but I landed. I also couldn't feel my foot after I did, and when I tried to walk, it didn't work. I managed to cut my hand also, which puzzles me to this day.

Well, look, sometimes life gets funny, and when you're not sure what to do, you climb the fence. If you fall and break your ankle, so be it. I managed to get in and out of the hospital with this thing that was drilled into my shin and underneath my foot, to make sure the bone would line up when it healed. Oh yeah, I checked my messages: I had gotten the job at Starbucks, and would start work on Monday. Talk about irony. This just seems to be the way life goes.

After falling all around my friends' house for a couple of weeks, getting back on my feet wasn't happening anytime soon. They were really tight on money, and I was always on their couch pretty much helpless, so they asked me to leave. I understood. I wasn't upset, it just sucked. I really don't know why we eventually stopped talking (me and those friends I stayed with). I get it, and I don't.

Those last few months I had been under a lot of stress, with people I knew getting shot, or killing themselves, others arrested. Getting phone calls and emails from people all over the world, as the law was starting to come down on them. Most of them found their way out, others were put out.

I was just destined to be miserable for the rest of my days, give or take a year. Back to being homeless, this time with a broken ankle and one hell of a story, that sounded better than, "I jumped a 12-foot fence to get to the other side." Take it or leave it, that's my story. A couple of centuries ago, I would have been a jester or a traveling sage.

Chapter 36
Philosophy and Experiences

People ask, "Why don't you work anymore?" It gets annoying trying to explain. I was meant for something better, and as far as I can tell, life goes haywire for me when I'm working. Money comes and goes, and the only truth that I've found in money is that it will get you stuff. Stuff that gets me into trouble, because I never know what to do with all the damn stuff. Stuff isn't important to me.

Now, good friends and a purpose in life: what more could any man really ask for? Yeah, I know, house and a car, and a wife with a pair kids sounds good. Well, look, I'm not sure what life has in store for me. I never really cared what was up ahead or behind me, I've always just preferred to live for the moment, because it's all the same, only the names really change.

I try not to make excuses for the way my life has gone, because then people think I'm upset with it all. I'm not; I have enjoyed my journey through the past 30 some-odd years, and I've made mistakes and paid dearly for them. I'm still standing firm that for being an outcast all my life, I lived a damn good life, and nobody can take that from me. I've got scars that tell stories people wish they had been present to see, while others cringe at the thought of the past.

I'm the type of guy to send a blank resume to a company, with a cover page and two blank sheets of paper, and then blame the company fax machine for it not turning out right. Why? To see their reaction, to see how they would react, and when they try to cover up the fact they didn't get the resume, it's party time. I WOULD RATHER DO NOTHING WITH A NOTION OF PURPOSE THAN WORK FOR NO OTHER PURPOSE THAN DOING NOTHING.

Yes, it's true, homeless people have come up to me and given me money, but I never asked. It's true, I would steal from my mother for a pack of cigarettes. After attending an alcohol awareness class as part of my probation, I realized that the only drug I'm addicted to is nicotine. As far as alcohol goes, while I don't know when to say when, I can go days, weeks, months, years without it. If you try to take my smokes, I will defend them like a she-gator protects her youngins'. I know my faults, and I have to live with them.

People say change, but what they mean is conform. Conform isn't something I do well, because at the end of the day when I go before God and try to defend my life, I don't want to use the excuse: "Well, so and so did it like this." That's a first-class ticket to Hell. I prefer to say, "Yeah, I screwed up, and I'm sorry. I tried not to do it again, but, you know, I tried to do right, but sometimes things don't go the way you plan them to."

I've lived a life that allowed me to see all of humanity and made me proud that I was nothing like most people. The definition of crazy in my book is doing something over and over again and getting the same results without a logical explanation. My mistakes in life were often done at moments in time that my logic supported the mistakes, and even though I knew they were wrong, I knew that I had to scratch off the wrong answers so that the right ones would become apparent. This method might not work for everybody, but I don't let fear guide me through life.

I don't fear death, nor do I fear life. Instead, I look forward to truth. While my methods broke laws, they led me towards the truth, and while I still consider my actions logical despite the fact they were and are illegal, I do not let laws of man act as guides for me to follow. I never have, and never will, for they are flawed just as men. Therefore, they don't really apply towards me deciding what I can and can't do.

The punishment must outweigh the benefits, but most of the time in most countries they don't. If you tell me selling drugs was wrong because you can go to jail, well, I'll keep selling drugs, because jail doesn't scare me. It's one of those places I'd prefer not to go, but I could make it work for me, so why should I fear it?

Now if you tell me selling crack is wrong because somebody might die from overdosing, I agree with you, and if I ever sold crack, I would stop. At the same time, if my life depended on selling and nobody would die from it as a direct result of me selling it to them, then damn right I'd move a kilo or two and move on with my life.

People say you can't live with anarchy, but that depends on the people, really. Most people are like sheep and will just do whatever it is they are told to do, so that they can have food, clothing, shelter, and whatever else floats their boats. I believe in self-reliance, but sometimes you have a skillset that allows you to barter your way through life. I can build my own house in the woods, I can hunt the same woods for food, I can sew my own clothes, but a good conversation with like-minded people happens to float my boat a little more than self-reliance does.

I crave interaction with people, despite sometimes not wanting to talk to people. It's only natural to seek interaction. Even if the reaction you seek is "Get away from me!", it's still a reaction. Otherwise, people would go off into the woods, and it would be like a tree falling where nobody could hear it: it wouldn't matter.

It's hard to tell people to be self-reliant in a city. It just is in a village mentality: self-reliance is selfish. In the woods by yourself, that's called survival. It just so happens you can survive in a village as well, but you must rely on others, the same as a big business man relies on the value of money versus the value of what he gets for it. To call him self-reliant because he has money is just foolish. To call him self-reliant because he is broke is a step up from foolish, but still not wise.

To judge a man on money is foolish; to judge him based on position is just as foolish. Now, is it wrong to cast judgment upon others? NO. It is, however, wrong to hold that judgment when you are proven wrong: that is what makes you an asshole. This troubles me, in the era when people have no real sense of what's right or wrong, only what's legal and what's illegal, or is it popular vs. uncool?

I myself will admit that what works for me won't work for others, and what works for them doesn't work for me. I'm different, some people say, that I think outside the box. That's not true: I think around the box. Sometimes in, sometimes out, sometimes on the border, but the difference in my thought process is I recognize the box, but don't acknowledge the box has any value other than its own inherent values. Meaning, if you put something in the box that is bigger than the box, I don't see how the box does any good, other than to say it's too small for my purposes.

I would much rather each person in the world have their own set of values and adhere to them than have a bunch of preset values for everyone that nobody can adhere to. To say my actions always adhere to my values would be a lie, but to say most of the time my actions and my values have been in line would be fairly accurate. If you don't live your life for yourself, what's the point? Don't go out on limb and think I just said you shouldn't give a damn about other people; what I said was don't live your life for others. If living your life in the service of others makes you happy, go for it.

I take the good, the bad, and the ugly known as life, but that doesn't mean I have to like it, nor do I accept it. I will fight the Man because I'm not the Man, and until I become the Man, we will both be thorns in each other's sides. I'm not a Republican or a Democrat: I hate all political parties, because they have the power to take the power from the people. What makes a man has nothing to do with wealth, station, or size of his guns, but rather his own personal worth and character. Some people will say my actions in life have shown me to be of a lesser breed of man BUT THEY WOULD BE WRONG. I have only ever claimed to a Survivalist™: I do what it takes to survive in the world we live in, where morals have no meaning, people care nothing for human life, nor do they understand the pursuit of knowledge. SO WHO THE HELL ARE THEY TO CALL ME A LESSER MAN?!

I hold firm to my belief that my quest for a sense purpose and meaning behind actions past, present, and future will give me closure and the ability to determine the best path for my own destiny. Despite the obstacles that will surely come, I shall continue to confront them head-on, because I don't acknowledge any man's authority over my own will to live a life in the manner that gives me the most sense of purpose. Regardless of how many obstacles life throws at me, I'll keep ducking, dodging, diving, and fighting all the challenges life has to offer, one after the next.

You can say what you want to about my first 30 years, but what the hell have you done with your life? I've been there and done that, I crossed off my bucket list before I reached 27, so you can take your criticism of me and shove it. They call me Jeff, but my NAME IS TENNESSEE.

Chapter 37
A Special Thank You

I would like to thank a variety of people for numerous things over the years and in no particular order. To put them in an order would be strange, for each of you have helped me so much over the years, and to rank it would be a disservice to what you've meant to me. To protect the innocent, and because I'm not sure if you'd want your names attached to this story for various reasons, I'll be using first names and nicknames.

To Quis, Dave, Wilson, Joe, Todd, Niece, Merrill, Mary, Joanne, Tyler, Mikey, Davis, Rooney, Sami, Dennis, Kim, Ace, K-Flex, Albert, Toni, Donna, Nikki, Lana, Jorge, Pencil Neck, Buster, Oleg, Hope, Julie, Joan, Willie, Jon, Marc, Jaque, and Romeo, thanks for showing me the ropes and lights of the town.

To Shaine, Blake, Scott, Carlos, Matt, Juan, Lorenzo, Clarence, Vlad, Rhee, Wendel, Moon Dawg, Pheng, and Trey, you guys helped me in ways that few would understand unless they were there, and you trusted me with many things. I owe a small part of what's left of my life to you guys.

To Bob, Lunch Box, John, Joel, Richard, Thomas, Grimace, Sung-G, Jacob, Adrian, Wally, Dave, Rhonda, Cooper, and Mika, you all got my back and saved my life at least once. For that, others will probably blame you for keeping me alive, but I for one thank you. Anywhere, anytime, anybody, just say the words, and it's done.

To John and Max, thanks so much for everything over the years. Max, you shouldn't read this for a couple more years, but all the same, thank you.

To Leslie, Antonia, Maria, Yaell, Efrat, Mia, Hope, Moran, Stacey, Leonora, Jackie, Dawn, Joanna, Jessica, Avery, Natasha, Nicole, and Lisa, ladies, your friendship meant more to me than anything else over the years. No matter what, I respected all of you for who you were, and I learned more about me because of you. I love you all, even if I didn't always show it.

To Kongo, my oldest, wisest, and most trusted friend, without you none of this would have been possible. Remember, they will come in masses from your left.

To Dan, Shimon, Simcha, Shmuel, Danny, Ezra, John, Lebi, Natan, Ephraim, and Benny Moskowitz, thanks for helping me find the balance in life I searched so hard for, and for being Good Men in times like these. We all need more men of high character in this world.

To Quattro, Jeff, Dennis, Eric, Tom, Layla, Angela, Megan, Kyle, Rodney, Casey, Kenny, Droopy, Dwight, Trey and Erica, we had some fun didn't we? It could have been worse, but somehow we are all still here.

To Scott, Dennis, Candice, Amy, Rodger, Margret, Bianca, Amanda, and Henry, you guys were the best and taught me lessons in telling a story through words and pictures. Without you guys, I would have had to draw this whole thing in crayons.

To Mrs. Meeks, thank you for calling me an illiterate prick in class. I do apologize for not reading <u>EVERYMAN</u>, but because of you, I went on to find a way to light some fires and scribble furiously towards a diploma or two, and prove a bunch of people wrong.

To all my cousins and extended family, you all have always been an inspiration in one way or another. Without you, I never would have made it to this point in my life.

I would also like to thank my parents, for finding a way to screw up my head enough in the developmental stages that as I aged was able to understand this cruel and twisted world, and also for teaching me the true meaning of insanity.

I would like to thank Todd and Rachel and the kids. You guys are family to me, and without y'all, I'd be sitting on a roof somewhere, howling at the moon, trying to find a way to express the anxiety and frustration of my past transgressions. Only through honesty and love can we find the true path to happiness.

To the Canadian goddess, and you know who you are, you were the best part of my day on many a dark day, when only the light of your beauty could dispel the clouds that covered my heart. I can't help but wonder about you; I still stand in awe before your beauty. I would have put you in the book, but to protect your virtue, I opted to only mention you now.

To my future ex-wife Lindsay Lohan, you ought to know I never believed the rumors, even on that cold, January morning when we first met. Having all the eyes on you when you walk into a room, trying to live up to the expectations of being the life of the party, I knew it wasn't easy. It never is, but sometimes you just have to say fuck it and go for the gold. Never look back, don't ever look back: it shows a guilty conscience. Instead, admit your mistakes and move forward, for you need not be ashamed of your past.

The only people ashamed of their past are those who consider themselves to be perfect, and those people are the ones with the darkest pasts. If you ever need a life coach, or just to talk like we used to, by all means, Call Me Tennessee at (901) 634-2132. I've been there and done that. Don't worry, I got your back.

Also to all my friends who are no longer with me, "Keep on rocking in the free world".

Now this one goes out to America, the land of the free and home of the brave. Only in such a place, can people of all nations collide and, true, your people look to Money like the Egyptians looked to Ra, Horus, Isis, Anubis, Seth, Hathor, Amun, and Geb, but it is still one of the places God had found a way to bless with some of the most majestic-looking places on Earth. For only in this country can men not be found guilty on the ramblings of a mad man and suspicions alone.

Yes, in America the presumed status is that of innocent, placing the burden of truth on the government. True, it makes it hard for real justice to be served, but nonetheless it's better than a place like Russia, where billions of dollars can't even buy you a trial. Yes, I would like thank the US of A for being a constant pest in the butt of the free peoples of China, N. Korea, Columbia, Cuba, Venezuela, Pakistan, Indonesia, Sudan, Iran, Iraq, Afghanistan, the UAE, Libya, Qatar, Mexico, Syria, Lebanon, Middle Earth, Saudi Arabia, Jordan, Yemen, Oman, and all of the break-away Russian republics. Yes, just to spite your enemies around the world, you pretend to be friends with those hardline socialists governments in Canada, England, France, Germany, and Portugal, to name a few.

In truth, you are waiting in the darkness to strike like a cobra at your true foes, the Greeks, Romans, and the citizens of Madagascar, for they are inherently evil beings. While it is true we still use the death penalty only in America, it is also true that the Supreme Court has upheld the rights of a suspected murderer to murder those coming to place him under false arrest. Only in America, can you move about freely from one city to the next one and find they have different laws that nobody seems to follow.

I know it's rough that in America we let women drive, unlike other Middle Eastern countries. We just assume that their lack of male genitalia has nothing to do with their sense of direction or ability to place a foot down on a pedal or two, or three. While it is true our kids are often undernourished, we don't force them to enlist in an army to get fed UN rice. I must give credit where credit is due: had it not been for a bunch of slave-owning, treasonous drunks who didn't like paying taxes, we would probably still be a colony.

While our revolution helped to bring down an empire, it was the French and Russian revolutions that taught the world how to bring down a monarchy and all those that supported the monarchs. While we have fought a few wars inside of our own borders, it has been a while since our army has opened fire upon our own citizens. While it's been a few years since a Vice President has been challenged to a duel over his own personal political views, at least we don't regularly kill the next in line to remind the next in line who is in the front of the line.

Yet still, it is a rare sight to see citizens dragged out of their homes, beaten and raped for holding hands with a male not in her own family at the age of 9. Oh wait my bad, that example isn't fair: because while she is a citizen, she is still property of her father. Upon reaching the age of 12, she can be sold to a gentleman as a wife. Then she is his property, and upon the age of 16, he can legally throw her on the streets without a dime, because she no longer pleases him in the marital bedroom. Like I said, that's just a bad example.

Perhaps we can look at another country to show us the way. How about China?! Nope, that one won't work either, because there if she has already had a child, she is forced to have an abortion or allow a local party official to determine her fate, which requires a bribe or sexual favors. That's also not the worst thing that could happen: if you and your wife were to get pregnant and then apply for the special birth permit, both would be either spayed or neutered after said abortion and, wait, I forgot, that's if you're lucky enough to not be executed by the state.

While it might be that in America they force you to get some sort of basic education that allows for most of its citizens to be, well, functionally illiterate, I mean it's not like China or India, where according to the test results from universities, the children are better educated. Did anybody else stop to ask how the kids have time to study when they are working legally at any age for less than the price of a doughnut in most countries? Could it be that the only children who are afforded the opportunity to learn how to read and write are from the haves and not the have-nots? I mean, it's not like they give a test to every 10 year-old in their countries to test their reading levels. What would happen if we only used the surveys of college graduates to determine the literacy rate in America?

At least people in America don't up and decide to protest high gas taxes by blowing up gas stations. Or every time the government runs out of money to just start printing ¥100 counterfeit bills, or just whenever we wanted our money to be worth more, we start selling counterfeit $100 to other countries to lower the value of the dollar. I mean, that would have to be in a country run by gangsters, or a short dictator with a stable of sex slaves.

Yes, America may be full of capitalists with no regard for human life, but I mean it's not like we continue to sell poisoned toys, lead paint, toxic drywall, contaminated baby formula, toothpaste with anti-freeze in it, poisoned dog food, tainted seafood, or prescription drugs with added chemicals to our trading partners! Just out of curiosity, where do those products go when American and European governments inform the uneducated Chinese government that the products are bad? I get the strange feeling they still get sold, or are used as tax write-offs in other countries.

Now, everybody would like to blame America for these problems. Me, I'm funny about this type of thing, I don't blame the government, but more the ideology of its people that decided for quantity over quality. Then I like to blame the people who manipulated the media and government officials to influence the poor people to buy the products. This is not to place the blame on rich and poor people, and the blame is not on the uneducated people or educated people. The blame is completely upon the people who buy the products thinking, "If it's cheaper, it must be better!"

The people who can't see the difference in whether they buy American or buy Wal-Mart, this is their problem. That's right: the people who are really to blame are the consumers who work for the corporations who opt to sell products that they buy from countries where people still die from the Plague. Think about that the next time you go grocery shopping: do you really want to buy lettuce from Mexico? Do you have any idea what kind of pesticides the growers use or have any faith in that government that randomly has prison guards staging prison breaks to let drugs dealers and pimps go free for a small fee?

Do you really trust that many people? I sure as Hell don't. Think for a minute or two every time you pick a product up, and ask yourself if you're sure about eating that or wearing clothing from that store. America is the greatest country on Earth; therefore, everybody is out to get us. To quote the Nature Boy Ric Flair, "To be the Man, You have to Beat the Man. WOOOOOO!!!" Yeah, I fight the Man at every turn, but the real question is why aren't you? Whose side are you on?

AT the END of the DAY, you know DAMN WELL I'm right. But who am I? Yeah, that's right just a guy that when he looks at the world and sees it for what it is, it makes me want a Cold Beer and a Joint to forget the fact I'm probably alone in this cruel unforgiving world. I'm American by birth, but Tennessean by the grace of GOD.

Jeff Klitzner, R.I.P. August 18th, 2011

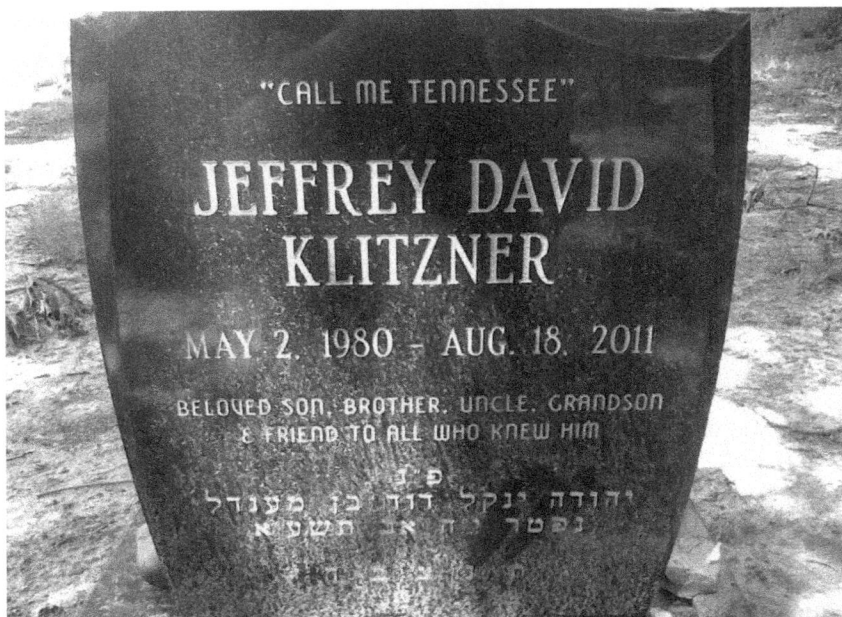

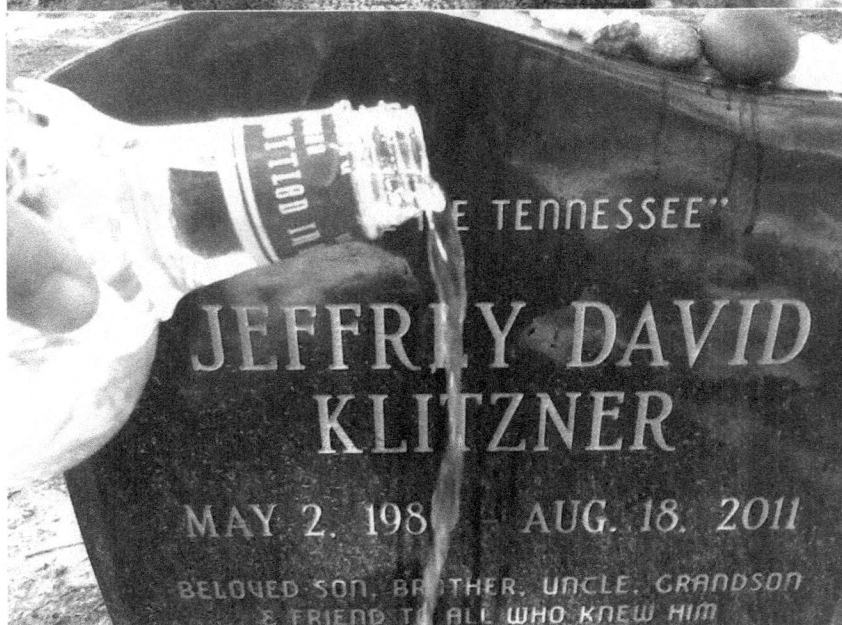

www.ingramcontent.com/pod-product-compliance
Lightning Source LLC
Chambersburg PA
CBHW032117040426
42449CB00005B/179